17 THE BEST OF NEWSPAPER DESIGN

CONTENTS

The Society of Newspaper Design
129 Dyer Street • Providence, RI 02903-3904
Judging takes place at The S.I. Newhouse School of Public Communications • Syracuse University • Syracuse, NY
FIRST PUBLISHED IN THE U.S.A. BY ROCKPORT PUBLISHERS, INC.

1996 SND OFFICERS

President
Jim Jennings
Design Consultant, Lexington, Ky

First Vice President
Neal Pattison
Seattle Post-Intelligencer

Second Vice President
Lynn Staley
Newsweek

Treasurer
Ed Kohorst
The Dallas Morning News

Secretary
Jean Moxam
Kansas City Star

Past President
Deborah Withey
Design Consultant, Knight-Ridder

The Society of Newspaper Design
Executive Director
Ray Chattman
Dave Gray (as of July 1, 1996)

The Society of Newspaper Design
129 Dyer Street
Providence, RI 02903-3904
Telephone: 401•276-2100
FAX: 401•276-2105

First published in the United States of America by:
Rockport Publishers, Inc.
146 Granite Street
Rockport, MA 01966
Telephone: 508•546-9590
Fax: 508•546-7141

Other distribution by:
Rockport Publishers, Inc.
Rockport, MA 01966

ISBN 1-56496-295-4 (Hardcover edition)
ISBN 1-878107-06-2 (Softcover edition)

10 9 8 7 6 5 4 3 2 1

Printed in China by Regent Publishing

BOOK CREDITS

Designer & Editor
C. Marshall Matlock
S.I. Newhouse School of Public Communications
Syracuse University

Associate Editor
Shamus Walker

Reproduction Photos
Bob Malish

SPECIAL THANKS

The S.I. Newhouse School of Public Communications
Syracuse University

Ray Chattman
Society of Newspaper Design

Nuri Ducassi
San Jose Mercury News

Barbara Hines
Howard University

Dale Peskin
Detroit News

JUDGING ASSISTANCE

Sheryl Cababa, James Carter, Holly Charron, Elaine Cipriano, Steve Dorsey, Carolyn Flynn, Kelly Frankeny, Marcie Gandell, Tara Gelsomino, Scott Goldman, Jesse Grimes, Barbara Hines, Scott Kober, Lucie Lacava, John Lahtinen, Phil Mahoney, Melvin Mason, Linda Monroe, Kenny Monteith, Jennifer Morey, Dale Peskin, Alisa Rivera, James Sackel, Alyson Salon, Becky Sample, Harris Siegel, Janis Sih, Heidi Smith, Kimberly Smith, Doug Van Reeth, Al Verone, Shamus Walker, Emily Zuzik

Introduction

It took five days, 21 judges and 35 assistants to sift through 9,615 entries from around the world to decide the winners in the 17th Best of Newspaper Design competition.

And after 220 hours of preparation and 58 hours of judging spread over those five days, judges issued 786 awards to 143 newspapers from the U.S. and 14 other countries.

Many of these winners are displayed in this book.

Judges use a complex system to decide winners. Balloting is secret; the system uses cups and chips so a judge does not know how others are voting until all votes are cast.

Almost as complex is the system to guard against conflicts of interest during the judging. Conflicts occurred when a judge came across an entry from his or her publication, a publication he or she had done recent consulting work for (recent is defined as an 18-month period immediately prior to judging) or a publication with which he or she directly competes. In these cases a "floating" judge was used to vote for or against the entry. A number of qualified "floating" judges were available on the judging floor to perform this duty.

Each panel consisted of five judges. At least three of them had to vote "yes" to grant an award. Entries receiving fewer than three votes were removed from the competition.
- Entries receiving three votes received an Award of Excellence.
- Entries receiving four or more votes in the first round advanced to the medal round.
- Entries receiving four votes during the medal round were awarded a Silver Medal.
- Entries receiving five votes (unanimous vote of the judging panel) earned a Gold Medal.
- At the end of competition judging, all judging panels came together to re-examine all Silver and Gold medal winners. Sometimes, when confronted with the entire body of medal winners (rather than winners from just one or two categories), judges will re-vote on the worthiness of some of their choices. Only the judges can move an entry up or down the awards scale.

SND presented three levels of awards.

An Award of Excellence was granted for work that was truly excellent. This award goes beyond mere technical or aesthetic competency. But to receive an award these entries need not be "perfect." It is appropriate to honor entries for such things as being daring and innovative if the entry is outstanding but less than 100 percent in every respect.

A Silver Medal was granted for work that went beyond excellence. The technical proficiency of the Silver Medal should stretch the limits of the medium. These entries are outstanding.

A Gold Medal was granted for work that defines the state of the art. Such an entry should stretch the limits of creativity. It should be impossible to find anything deficient in a gold-winning entry. It should be near perfect. Ten Gold Medals were awarded in the 17th Edition judging.

In addition to the Award of Excellence, Silver and Gold medals, two special honors are possible: the Judges' Special Recognition and the Best of Show. These honors are given only when specific, special circumstances warrant the awards.

A Judges' Special Recognition can be awarded by a team of judges or by all judges for work that is outstanding in an area not necessarily singled out by the Award of Excellence, Silver or Gold award structure. This recognition has been granted for such things as use of photography, use of informational graphics and the use of typography throughout a body of work. This body of work may be a particular publication, section or sections by an individual or staff. The special recognition does not supplant any Award of Excellence, Silver or Gold and should be seen as an adjunct. Six JSRs where awarded in the 17th Edition competition.

Best of Show is the best of the Gold Medal winners. Discussion for this award takes place at the conclusion of the judging. Judges have an opportunity to view all Silver and Gold winners at the same time. There is no limit as to the number of Best of Show awards that may be presented in one or more categories; however, in the past such awards were non-existent or very few in number. One Best of Show was given in the 17th Edition judging.

C. Marshall Matlock
Competition Committee Chair

Introducción

Se requirieron cinco días, 21 jueces y 35 auxiliares, para examinar a los 9.615 participantes procedentes del mundo entero, con el fin de escoger los ganadores del Duodécimo Concurso de Formato de Periódicos.

Y, tras 220 horas de preparación y 58 horas de juicio que abarcaron esos cinco días, los jueces concedieron 786 premios a 143 periódicos de los E.E. U.U. y de otros 14 países.

En este libro se muestran muchos de estos ganadores.

Los jueces utilizan un sistema complejo, para escoger a los ganadores. La votación es secreta, por medio de urnas y fichas, de manera que los jueces no saben cómo votaron los demás, mientras no se depositen todos los votos.

Casi igualmente complejo es el sistema de protección contra los conflictos de intereses durante el juicio. Los conflictos surgieron cuando un juez tropezó con un trabajo de su propia publicación, de una publicación a la cual había asesorado recientemente ("recientemente" se define como el período de 18 meses, inmediatamente anterior al juicio), o con una publicación con la cual competía directamente. En estos casos se utilizó un juez "flotante," para votar por el trabajo o contra él. En la sala del juicio hubo varios jueces "flotantes" idóneos, disponibles para cumplir esta función.

Cada panel estuvo integrado por cinco jueces. Por lo menos tres de ellos debían votar "sí," para conceder un premio. Los trabajos que recibieron menos de tres votos, fueron excluidos del concurso.
- Los trabajos que obtuvieron tres votos, recibieron un premio de excelencia.
- Los trabajos que recibieron cuatro votos o más en la primera ronda, avanzaron hasta la de las medallas.
- Los trabajos que obtuvieron cuatro votos durante la ronda de las medallas, recibieron medalla de plata.
- Los trabajos que obtuvieron cinco votos (voto unánime de los jueces), ganaron medallas de oro.
- Al final del juicio del concurso todos los paneles de jueces se reunieron, para estudiar nuevamente a todos los ganadores de medallas de plata y de oro. A veces, al enfrentarse a la totalidad de los ganadores de medallas (en vez de los ganadores de apenas una o dos categorías), los jueces votarán nuevamente sobre los méritos de algunos de los trabajos escogidos por ellos. Sólo los jueces pueden asignar una categoría superior o inferior a un trabajo, dentro de la escala de premios.

SND concedió tres niveles de premios

Se concedió un premio de excelencia a los trabajos realmente excelentes. Este premio va más allá de la mera competencia técnica o estética. Pero para recibir un premio, no es necesario que estos trabajos participantes sean "perfectos." Es correcto conceder honores por cosas tales como la osadía y la innovación, si el trabajo es notable, pero inferior al 100 por ciento en todos los aspectos.

Se concedió una medalla de plata a los trabajos superiores a la excelencia. La habilidad técnica debe forzar los límites del medio. Estos trabajos son notables.

Se concedió una medalla de oro, por trabajos que definen los avances más recientes. Un trabajo tal debe hacer retroceder los límites de la creatividad. Debe ser imposible hallar cualquier deficiencia en un trabajo ganador de medalla de oro. Debe ser casi perfecto. En el juicio de la decimoséptima edición, se concedieron diez medallas de oro.

Además de los premios de excelencia y las medallas de plata y oro, se conceden dos premios especiales: el de reconocimiento especial de los jueces y el de mejor del evento. Estos premios se conceden únicamente cuando lo justifican determinadas circunstancias especiales.

El premio de reconocimiento especial de los jueces puede concederse por un grupo de jueces o por todos ellos, por trabajos notables en un área no necesariamente destacada por la estructura de los premios de excelencia y de las medallas de plata y oro. Este reconocimiento se ha concedido por razones tales como la utilización de la fotografía, la utilización de las gráficas informativas y la de la tipografía en el conjunto de una obra. Este conjunto puede ser una publicación, o una o varias secciones específicas, por una persona o por todo el personal. El reconocimiento especial no reemplaza a ningún premio de excelencia ni medalla de oro o plata, y debe considerarse como adicional. En la decimoséptima edición del concurso, se concedieron seis premios de reconocimiento especial de los jueces.

El mejor del evento, es el mejor de los ganadores de medallas de oro. La discusión de este premio se efectúa al concluir el juicio. Los jueces tienen la oportunidad de examinar simultáneamente a todos los ganadores de medallas de plata y oro. No hay ningún límite respecto al número de premios al mejor del evento, que pueden concederse en una o varias categorías. No obstante, antiguamente tales premios no existían o eran muy contados. En el juicio de la decimoséptima edición, se concedió un premio al mejor del evento.

C. Marshall Matlock
Presidente del Comité del Concurso

Foreword

I call it "The art of newspapers." The cover of this book is based on a favorite work of art, Georges Seurat's Sunday on La Grande Jatte. The painting — a mesmerizing example of impressionism — explores community, the diversity of life, and a sense of a unique place in a unique time. It uses thousands of tiny, colored dots to create a story.

So what has this to do with newspapers?

Each dot in the painting, like each word or bit of data in a newspaper, coveys information, imparts ideas. The artist creates an image, tells a story, one dot at a time. That is the art of painting. It is also the art of newspapers.

Each February in a large auditorium in Syracuse, New York, the Society of Newspaper Design and the S.I. Newhouse School of Public Communications at Syracuse University create a similar canvass — The Best of Newspaper Design. This year, about 250 newspapers from 24 nations participated, submitting nearly 10,000 entries.

Many believe that competition — a rivalry for a prize — brings so many newspapers to Syracuse in the cold of winter. I believe there is a more powerful attraction. The Best of Newspaper Design is an exhibition of excellence. Designers enter to celebrate their work as storytellers. Their entries demonstrate how powerfully they succeed.

Competition is, however, integral to this exhibition. It provides a standard to measure quality, creativity and progress. In painstaking judging punctuated by lively discussion and agonizing debate, 21 judges from five countries evaluated how newspapers used design to communicate ideas. Over five days, they selected pages, photographs, graphics and illustrations that best represent the art of newspapers. Those selections are represented in this book.

An important part of the judging was the selection of the World's Best-Designed Newspapers. This was no mere beauty contest. Editors and designers evaluated content, not just design, from mandatory dates representing typical, daily coverage. Judges chose 22 of the world's newspapers — 11 from the United States, 11 from North America, South America and Europe — as distinguished examples of how newspapers use content and design to tell important stories and reach readers.

None of this would have happened without the dedication and hard work of many people. Once again, Marshall Matlock, Shamus Walker and the students and administration of Syracuse University ensured that a complex exercise was executed flawlessly. Ray Chattman provided steadfast guidance and experience from SND's executive office, while SND president Jim Jennings allowed the kind of creativity and risk-taking that enabled the contest to grow and flourish. Kelly Frankeny, Scott Goldman, Carolyn Flynn, Harris Siegel and other volunteers brought direction and efficiency to what many regard as the best-run contest in the newspaper industry.

But mostly it was the judges that defined this contest. Their task — to distinguish a small percentage of a body of distinguished work — was daunting. They accomplished this task with leadership, judgment, fairness and high regard for craft.

The art of newspapers was well-served. The real winners were the readers of our newspapers.

Dale Peskin
17th Edition Coordinator

Preámbulo

Yo lo llamo "El arte de los periódicos." La cubierta de este libro se basa en una popular obra de arte de Georges Seurat: Domingo en La Grande Jatte. La pintura, una muestra fascinante del impresionismo, explora la comunidad, la diversidad de la vida y un sentido de ubicación única dentro de un momento único. Se vale de miles de puntitos de colores, para narrar una historia.

Y, ¿qué tiene que ver todo esto con los periódicos?

Cada punto de la pintura, como cada palabra o dato de un periódico, transmite información y divulga ideas. El artista crea una imagen, narra una historia punto por punto. Ese es el arte de la pintura. También es el arte de los periódicos.

Cada febrero, en un vasto auditorio en Syracuse, Nueva York, la Sociedad de Diseño de Periódicos y la Escuela S.I. Newhouse de Comunicaciones Públicas de la Universidad de Syracuse, crean un lienzo similar: el Mejor Diseño de Periódico. Este año participaron aproximadamente 250 periódicos de 24 naciones, que sometieron cerca de 10.000 trabajos.

Muchos creen que el concurso, la rivalidad por un premio, atrae tantos periódicos a Syracuse en lo más frío del invierno. Yo creo que existe una atracción más poderosa: el Mejor Diseño de Periódico es un despliegue de excelencia. Los diseñadores participan para celebrar su trabajo de narradores. Sus trabajos demuestran el poder narrativo que alcanzan.

No obstante, la competencia forma parte integrante de este despliegue. Proporciona una norma de medición de la calidad, la creatividad y el progreso. En un esmerado juicio salpicado de animadas discusiones y debates agotadores, 21 jueces procedentes de cinco países evaluaron la forma en la cual los periódicos utilizaban el diseño para comunicar ideas. Durante cinco días escogieron las páginas, fotografías, gráficas e ilustraciones que mejor representaban el arte de los periódicos. Los trabajos escogidos se encuentran representados en este libro.

Una parte importante del juicio, fue la elección de los periódicos mejor diseñados del mundo. No fue un mero concurso de belleza. Los editores y los diseñadores evaluaron el contenido, no sólo el diseño, en fechas obligatorias, que representaban la típica cobertura diaria. Los jueces escogieron a 22 de los periódicos del mundo, 11 de los Estados Unidos, 11 de América del Norte, América del Sur y Europa, como ejemplos distinguidos de la forma en la cual los periódicos utilizan el contenido y el diseño para narrar importantes historias y llegar a los lectores.

Nada de esto habría ocurrido sin la dedicación y el trabajo intenso de muchas personas. Una vez más, Marshall Matlock, Shamus Walker y los estudiantes y la administración de la Universidad de Syracuse garantizaron que un complejo ejercicio se ejecutara en forma impecable. Ray Chattman ofreció una orientación y una experiencia constantes desde la oficina ejecutiva de SND, mientras Jim Jennings, Presidente de SND, permitía la clase de creatividad y atrevimiento que hicieron posible que el concurso prosperara y floreciera. Kelly Frankeny, Scott Goldman, Carolyn Flynn, Harris Siegel y los demás voluntarios, imprimieron dirección y eficiencia a lo que muchos consideran el concurso mejor organizado de la industria periodística.

Pero, más que todo fueron los jueces quienes decidieron este concurso. Su tarea, destacar un pequeño porcentaje de un conjunto de trabajos distinguidos, fue sobrecogedora. Y al cumplirla dieron pruebas de liderazgo, criterio, justicia y un gran respeto hacia la profesión.

El arte de los periódicos quedó bien servido. Los verdaderos ganadores fueron los lectores de nuestros periódicos.

Dale Peskin
Coordinador de la decimoséptima edición

1

The Word's Best-Designed Newspapers excel at presenting the news. Judges were asked to evaluate, compare and discuss the papers entered in this category. Newspapers were evaluated on the quality of the writing, storytelling, execution, photography, headlines and design.

World's Best-Designed Newspapers

- Best of Show
- Judges' Special Recognition

The Daily Telegraph
London, England

How does one select something that will be known forever as the "world's best"? How can one apply that to the ever-changing landscape of the world's newspapers? And whom does one find to make such a distinction?

The Society of Newspaper Design once again assembled an international panel of top newspaper editors and handed it a most difficult chore: find the World's Best-Designed Newspapers.

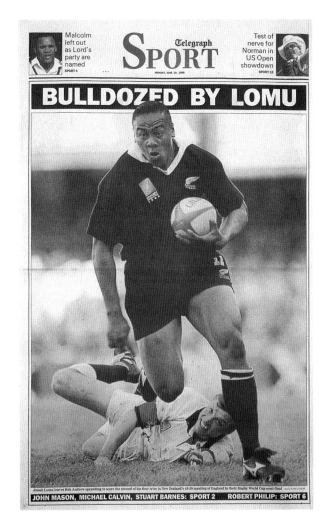

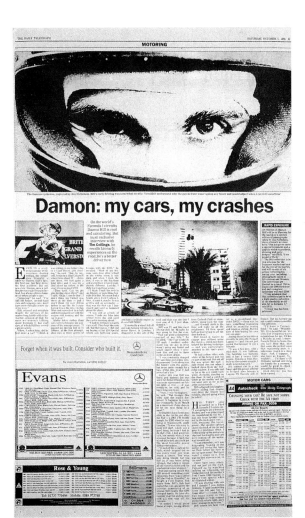

The Detroit News
Detroit, MI

¿Cómo escoge uno algo que se conocerá para siempre como "el mejor del mundo"? ¿Cómo puede uno aplicar esa expresión al siempre variable panorama de los periódicos del mundo? Y ¿a quién puede encontrarse para que haga tal diferenciación?

La Sociedad de Diseño de Periódicos reunió una vez más a un panel internacional de los principales editores de periódicos, y le confió una tarea dificilísima: la de encontrar los periódicos mejor diseñados del mundo.

Accent

New Chicago exhibit shows outdoor-lover Claude Monet as light years ahead of his time

lasting impressions

Sports

Time to show some patience

McKinney deserves a chance to play out his five-year plan . . . with clout

Jordan sets tone

Chicago icon scores 29, big men inflict damage without Pippen as Bulls pull away in second half.

Big names missing from Tigers lineup

Replacements have not returned, but many regulars will not play in initial week of short spring season.

Cochran vs. Clark made great courtroom drama

Business

Flint entrepreneur turns scrap plastic into thriving business

Saturn: It's one of a kind

No other auto company invites its customers over for ribs, car chat

Saturn fine-tuned for '96; no revolutionary changes

Infrared device used on airplanes may soon help detect breast cancer

Saturn's trademark value, service add up to this car's appeal

The Globe and Mail
Toronto, Canada

As a criteria, judges looked not at the revolving door that is the day's news, but rather at those things on a newspaper that do not change: its character, its sense of community, its attention to detail, the attitude with which it conveys information and its use of resources in a time when the resource pool at many newspapers is being drained.

Moreover, judges looked at the fundamental element of a newspaper: how it tells stories.

La Vanguardia
Barcelona, Spain

Como criterio rector, los jueces examinaron, no la puerta giratoria que son las noticias del día, sino aquellas cosas inmutables en un periódico: su carácter, su sentido comunitario, su atención a los detalles, la actitud con la cual transmite la información y su utilización de los recursos, en una época en la cual se está agotando el conjunto de los recursos de muchos periódicos.

Además, los jueces examinaron los elementos fundamentales de un periódico: cómo narra sus historias.

• Also Award of Excellence for Informational Graphics

The New York Times
New York, NY

Twenty-two newspapers from seven countries were named as the World's Best-Designed Newspapers. Eight were in the 175,000 and above circulation division; seven were in the 50,000 through 174,999 circulation bracket; and seven were in the 49,999 circulation or less.

From the El Observador in Montevideo, Uruguay and the TimesDaily in Florence, Ala. to The Daily Telegraph in London, England and the Saint Paul (Minn.) Pioneer Press, these 22 newspapers shared an expert understanding of their audiences and newspaper fundamentals. And now they share a title of the World's Best-Designed Newspapers.

The Oregonian
Portland, OR

Veintidós periódicos de siete países, fueron escogidos como los periódicos mejor diseñados del mundo. Ocho se encontraban en la categoría de una circulación de 175.000 ejemplares y más; siete, en la categoría de circulación de 50.000 a 174.999 ejemplares, y siete se encontraban en la categoría de circulación de 49.999 ejemplares o menos.

Desde El Observador, de Montevideo, Uruguay y el TimesDaily en Florence, Alabama, hasta The Daily Telegraph, en Londres, Inglaterra y el Pioneer Press de Saint Paul, Minnesota, estos 22 periódicos tuvieron en común un conocimiento experto de sus lectores y de las nociones fundamentales de lo que es un periódico. Y hoy comparten el título de periódicos mejor diseñados del mundo.

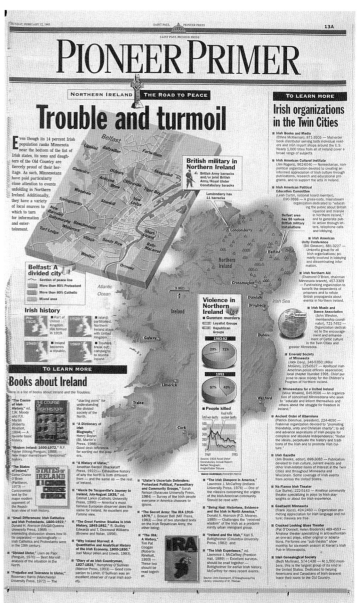

Saint Paul Pioneer Press
St Paul, MN

"One of the things that distinguishes all these newspapers is that they are very in touch with their readers," said Marty Petty, senior vice president and general manager, The Hartford (Conn.) Courant. "Almost without exception, these papers seem to have a good sense of place, a sense of what their readers want and a sense of their mission."

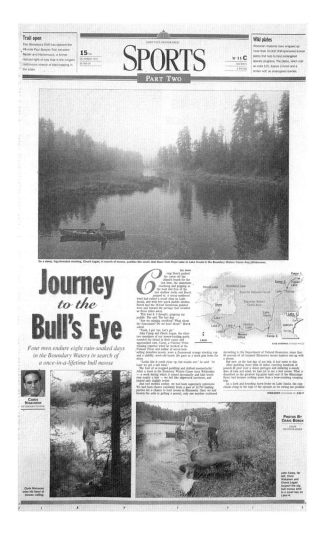

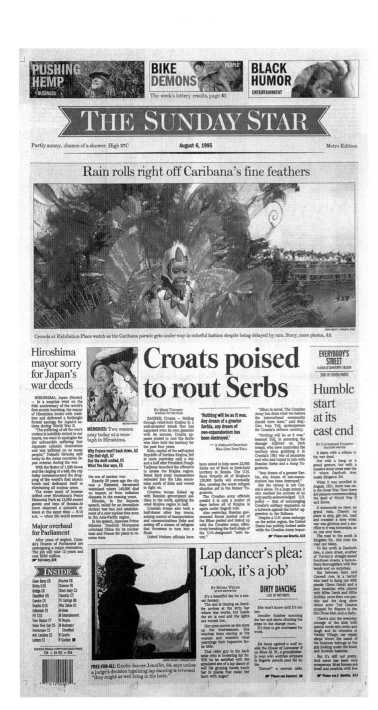

The Toronto Star
Toronto, Canada

"Una de las cosas que distinguen a todos estos periódicos, es que se están en contacto con sus lectores," dijo Marty Petty, vicepresidente principal y gerente general de The Hartford Courant (Connecticut). "Casi sin excepción, estos periódicos parecen tener un buen sentido de la oportunidad, un sentido de lo que desean sus lectores y un sentido de su misión."

FYI

Sunday, June 18, 1995 Page B8

Good fences, good neighbors

By Jennifer Jones

DIVIDING LINES

BOULEVARD PARKING

ENCROACHMENT PERMIT

OTHER ENCROACHMENTS

Driveway parking, widening

FENCING YOURSELF IN

YOUR PROPERTY LINE

CALL BEFORE YOU DIG

PEOPLE

FYI · HAVE YOUR SAY · PUZZLES · STARSHIP   Sunday, August 6, 1995 Section C

Cycling demons

Local cyclists Joe Dias and Tommy Quesnel are the top two prospects in the World Cycle Messengers Championship set for next weekend in Toronto

By Peter Cheney

'COOL RIDER': Joe Dias, who placed 82nd in last year's championship in Berlin, brings to the tap-tap courier game a professional dedication, even though there's no money in it.

MADE ON WHEELS: At same future date Mississauga-born Tommy Quesnel would like to work with mountain tools, but for now bikes are the epicentre of his life. He placed 14th in the Berlin race.

"You have the friends, and you can look the way you want when countering. You know, rebel without a clue."

SPORTS

Sunday, January 22, 1995 Section C

SUNDIN SCORES: Mats Sundin pokes puck into net for his first goal as a Leaf after nice feed from Doug Gilmour last night to put the Leafs ahead 1-0 early in game.

Sharks devour Leaf rookie

Jonsson struggles to find NHL legs in loss to San Jose

By Damien Cox

Sharks 3, Leafs 2

Inside . . .

PLAY BALL! While Robbie Alomar, seen yesterday trying to avoid a sliding Bob Natal, is playing winter ball, others are trying to take his spot on the Jays...

Jays' Florida follies attract dreamers from far and wide

DUNEDIN, Fla. (AP)

SPOTLIGHT

ENTERTAINMENT · PEOPLE · TELEVISION   Sunday, January 22, 1995 Section B

New MuchMusic veejay Sook-Yin Lee knows how to use her noodle in wacky world of performance art

By Jennie Punter

The cutting Wedge

GRAND EXPERIMENTER: After enough careers-in-the-making to last others a lifetime, Sook-Yin Lee has a cool gig with her musical 'fireside chats' beaming coast-to-coast on MuchMusic's The Wedge and Videoflow.

Her refreshing approach has drawn passionate, traffic-stopping support from fans

'The Fighting Motts' spice up talk radio

By Mira Friedlander

OPPOSITE: 'Inflammatory' Paul Mott balanced by "more sensitive" Carol.

Diario 16
Madrid, Spain

"Another thing is that all (newspapers) seem to be going out of their way to be helpful to readers: multiple entry points into stories, information in digestible chunks. In a highly time constrained society, these papers are working much harder to keep their readers interested," said Peter Bhatia, managing editor, The Oregonian, Portland, Ore.

ARTE El Congreso pide al Gobierno un estatuto para el Museo Reina Sofía

Madrid.—El Congreso pidió ayer al Gobierno asuma el informe de fiscalización del Museo Reina Sofía realizado por el Tribunal de Cuentas, una de cuyas recomendaciones era la de la creación de un estatuto. El informe detectó recuentos deficientes de las ventas de entradas y dudoso precedimiento en el inventario de catálogos, y acordó solicitar el inventario de las obras y depósitos del Reina Sofía. EFE

ARTE Hans Haacke expone la Fundación Tàpies de Barcelona

Barcelona.—El artista alemán Hans Haacke es el protagonista de la exposición Obra social en la Fundación Tàpies de Barcelona en la que se presentan ejemplos de sus diferentes períodos creativos, centrados en la crítica social e institucional. En ella critica la utilización del arte con el poder. La Caixa y las relaciones del arte con el poder.
XAVIER GAFAROT

LIBROS La editorial Plaza y Janés ficha a Rafael Borràs

Madrid.—Rafael Borràs fue presentado anoche en una fiesta como asesor de la editorial Plaza y Janés. Barcelona de 59 años ha trabajado en Planeta cargo que abandonó por la que edificio de "despido improcedente", tras ser indemnizado. D18

CULTURA 16

A CONTRACORRIENTE Emile Cioran logró despertar el interés de sus inesperados lectores por su desprecio hacia las grandes teorías, hacia los sistemas en boga interrogando los sueños hacia una vigilia sin fin.

Ciorán se enfrentó a la muerte

Desaparece el máximo exponente de la filosofía de la negación y el mejor discípulo de Nietzsche

JACOBO MACHOVER
París

Hacía varios meses que Cioran no abandonaba su cama de hospital aquejado por la enfermedad de Alzheimer. El rumano más secreto de París, el filósofo de la duda, el motor del aforismos llenos de humor, de pesimismo y de lucidez acaba de morir, a la edad de 84 años, en la ciudad que había elegido desde 1937 como base de su exilio permanente.

DATOS

Emile M. Cioran nace en Rumanía en 1911. Residía exiliado en Francia desde 1937. Escribió obras como *Ese maldito yo*, *De lágrimas y de santos*, *Historia y utopía*, *Silogismos de la amargura*, *Ejercicios de admiración*, *La caída en el tiempo*, *El ocaso del pensamiento* y *Del inconveniente de haber nacido*.

nente. Emil Cioran vivía en el barrio Latino, en una buhardilla de la rue de l'Odeon, rehuía las entrevistas y los medios de comunicación, así como los contactos con los ambientes intelectuales, excepto con su compatriota Eugène Ionesco, otro ilustre rumano de París. Pocos días antes de su muerte, sin embargo, la editorial Gallimard publicaba un libro de entrevistas de Cioran, realizadas por Michael Jakob, que cobra

Lo que le importaba al filósofo rumano eran los creadores que lindaban con la locura

ahora un carácter casi póstumo. Cioran escribía en francés, después de haber abandonado para siempre su país y su lengua materna. Antes, a los 22 años, había escrito su primer libro, *En la cumbre de la desesperación*, que el consideraba como su testamento porque, decía, "pensaba que me iba a suicidar". En Rumanía, Cioran empezó a vivir de noche. "Todo lo que he escrito, todo lo que he pensado, todo lo que he elaborado, to-

das mis divagaciones encuentran su origen en esas dramas: alrededor de los 20 años, perdí el sueño." De esa nocheuen vela, Cioran extrae la materia de su delirio, sus reflexiones sobre el mismo la violencia, sobre el misticismo. Es el tiempo discontinuo, sin interrupción, las treguas para el pensamiento. El escritor nunca vivió como vivo el común de los mortales.

Existió poseído de una melancolía permanente

Sigue en pág. siguiente

R. Madrid - Ajax

El Campeón de Europa defenderá en Chamartín el liderato en el grupo D

Las alineaciones

R. Madrid	Ajax
Buyo 1	Van der Sar
Chendo 2	Reiziger
Alkorta 4	Bogarde
Sanchís 5	Blind
Quique 3	Reuser
Luis Enrique 9	Kluivert
Redondo 6	Litmanen
Laudrup 10	Davids
Amavisca 11	Overmars
Raúl 7	R. de Boer
Zamorano 9	Finidi
Sandro 12	Silooy
Cañizares 13	Grim
Nando 14	Musampa
Michel 15	Wooter
Milla 16	Karu

Árbitro
Helmut Krug (Alemania)
A las 20.30, por TVE-1
Taquilla, 120 millones

Las claves

La posesión del balón
Si el Real Madrid consigue adueñarse de la pelota habrá desarmado el potencial de los actuales campeones de Europa, que está acostumbrado a derrotar a los contrarios con el balón como permanente aliado

La creatividad de Laudrup
El jugador danés puede romper, con la constante ayuda de Raúl, el sólido sistema defensivo holandés. El Real Madrid tiene que aprovechar su habitual media hora de buen fútbol para intentar llevarse el partido.

El juego por las bandas del Ajax
El campeón holandés rompe las defensas de sus contrarios con las entradas por las bandas de Finidi y Overmars. Si el Madrid consigue taponar esa vía de penetración tendrá mucho ganado.

Zamorano
El chileno se ha convertido, junto a Raúl, en el soporte ofensivo del Real Madrid en la Liga de Campeones. Su capacidad de presión sobre la defensa rival y el remate de cabeza son los atributos que pueden tumbar al Ajax. Durante su reciente lesión, Esnáider consiguió que el equipo de Cioran funcionara bien. Se entiende muy bien con Amavisca y con Raúl.

Overmars
Es uno de los futbolistas de más calidad del fútbol holandés. Extremo a la vieja usanza, utiliza las dos piernas, aunque abusa ocupa la demarcación de Brian Roy abandonó el Ajax. Es muy rápido y hábil en el regate y tiene un certero remate. En el partido de ida fue el autor del gol.

El partido de ida

Ajax - Real Madrid: (1 - 0)
> 40.000 espectadores
> Gol: Overmars (14')
> Árbitro: M. Ceccrini (Italia)
> Amonestados:
> Wooter (79') por el Ajax
> Zamorano (70') por el Madrid

S i alguien creyó que el estado militar en América Latina se había convertido en un 'fantasma' del pasado, los recientes acontecimientos en Perú y Chile vienen a demostrar que el 'oso' estaba agazapado, pero no dormido.

MUNDO 16

EL NAVEGANTE

① Perú
② Chile
③ Angola

ADOLFO SALVADOR

Moscú agacha la cabeza

Los chechenos logran un compromiso de alto el fuego

Moscú.—Los rebeldes chechenos que se mantienen fuertes en el interior del hospital de Budienovsk con 1.000 rehenes en su poder consiguieron a las dos de la pasada madrugada (hora española) el compromiso del primer ministro Ruso, Víctor Chernomyrdin, de suspender las hostilidades en la república independentista a cambio de la liberación de los rehenes.

Tras una jornada en la que se produceron dos ataques de comandos rusos contra los rebeldes liderados por Shamil Bassayev con el mayor resultado de un par de centenares de rehenes liberados, la radical actitud del comando checheno obligó a las autoridades rusas a buscar un compromiso negociado que se materializó mediante conversaciones telefónicas.

El principio de acuerdo pone fin a una tensa jornada de escaramuzas. Tras el ataque frustrado de Rusia, los rebeldes independentistas reanudaron las negociaciones con las autoridades federales, que se refirieron a haber conseguido la liberación de unas 227 personas entre rehenes rusos.

La decisión de atacar fue objeto de polémica, ya que

nadie en Moscú había dado la orden en tal sentido. La responsabilidad fue finalmente asumida por el presidente ruso, Boris Yeltsin, desde la localidad canadiense de Halifax donde mantuvo contactos con los jefes de Estado y Gobierno de los siete países más industrializados del planeta (G-7).

"La decisión había sido tomada después de que nos reuniera con mis ministros, inmediatamente antes de partir hacia Halifax," comentó Yeltsin. Sin embargo, la reacción entre las autoridades civiles y militares en Moscú fue de sorpresa ante el inicio del primer asalto, que se produjo en la madrugada de ayer. De hecho, los primeros portavoces oficiales se refalaron que las tropas de elite actuaron "de manera emocional" cuando escucharon que se producían disparos, gritos de los rehenes y órdenes tajantes de los checenos. Entre los rehenes obligados a primera fila murieron cinco soldados, la mayoría, rehenes obligados a primera fila del hospital, la mayoría, rehenes obligados a primera fila.

BOSNIA

Las tropas fieles a Izetbegovic alcanzan Pale con dos misiles

PERÚ

Consternación en todo el país por la excarcelación de decenas de militares

CHILE

Denuncian que el Ejército se ha puesto al borde de la ley por ayudar a Contreras

ALBERTO FUJIMORI

HACIA LA SALVACIÓN Un soldado ruso protege a una enfermera y a un niño, liberados durante el primer ataque. Ciento sesenta rehenes fueron salvados por la acción armada.

Crónica del enviado especial de D16 en la página siguiente

inocentes. **2. Como era de esperar, el pulso en Chile entre el poder civil y el militar se encuentra en su momento álgido.** Pinochet, que ha jugado con varias cartas, ha puesto de 'acatar' la sentencia contra su jefe de la DINA, el general Manuel Contreras, a colocar al Ejército al borde de la legalidad', según las versiones más ateres, con la protección en desagrado ofrecida al que fuera mero ejecutor de sus órdenes. Mientras tanto, el poder civil asiste impotente al espectáculo de unos militares que se están burlando abiertamente de la justicia. **3. La crisis angoleña parece definitivamente encauzada después de que el gobernante Movimiento de Liberación haya aceptado la presencia del líder guerrillero Jonas Savimbi en la vicepresidencia del Gobierno. Ya sólo falta que se concrete y que Dos Santos y Savimbi puedan trabajar juntos por el futuro de Angola.**

Bolsa de Madrid	Índice Ibex	Cotización marco	Cotización dólar	Cotización ecu
306,3	**3.368**	**85,75**	**120,48**	**159,13**
-0,12	-0,24			

El mercado madrileño cerró ayer con un leve recorte en la mayoría de las cotizaciones, derivadas de las tópicas recogidas de las plusvalías tras las fuertes ganancias de días anteriores.

La moneda española continuó ayer su fortalecimiento con el dólar estadounidense y con el marco alemán, aunque con menos fuerza que el día anterior. En el mercado secundario de deuda los precios siguieron la senda de la recuperación iniciada esta semana a la vez que se vieron propiciada por la mejora de los activos financieros alemanes.

ECONOMIA 6

INCIDENTES EN SEVILLA Trabajadores de la factoría de Astilleros Españoles en Sevilla quemaron ayer neumáticos y cortaron el tráfico frente a las puertas del Parlamento andaluz

El Gobierno, inflexible, aplicará el ajuste naval pese al rechazo unánime

Eguiagaray dice que "hay 45.000 razones" mientras en Sevilla y Cádiz surgen incidentes

Madrid-Sevilla / D16.–El Gobierno se mostró ayer tajante en la aplicación del Plan Estratégico de Competitividad diseñado para los astilleros españoles, que supondrá la pérdida de 5.100 empleos y el cierre de las factorías de Sevilla y Cádiz, entre otras medidas.

Eguiagaray señaló a EP Televisión que hay 45.000 buenas razones para justificar el ajuste, en referencia a los problemas del sector. El ministro indicó que "se comprende que los trabajadores que tienen inquietudes por su futuro protesten", pero sin embargo, es necesario establecer plazos flexibles que permitan la presentación de una alternativa, con el objetivo de mediar sus aspectos más regresivos del ajuste.

CC OO ADVIERTE

CC OO advirtió ayer que habrá movilizaciones en todos los astilleros públicos si la DCN no flexibiliza el plan de reconversión naval y Cádiz.

se expresan, a veces, en términos muy duros".

Javier Salas, presidente del INI, afirmó que el plan que se va a aprobar "es el único encima de la mesa", pero tras descartó la posibilidad de suavizar el ajuste tras las protestas.

Salas dijo que éstas se encuentran "dentro de las reglas del juego", y respecto al plazo para presentar una alternativa por las principales calles de la ciudad como protesta contra el PEC del sector.

período de negociación.
Los primeros incidentes asomaron ayer. En Cádiz, unos 300 trabajadores de Astilleros cortaron el tráfico y quemaron neumáticos ante las puertas del sector. Mientras tanto, en Cádiz, cerca de 4.000 trabajadores de Astilleros Españoles de Cádiz y Puerto Real se manifestaron por las principales calles de la ciudad.

El consejero de Industria de la Xunta de Galicia, Antonio Couceiro, apuntó por su parte

la necesidad de acometer un último ajuste en el sector naval, aunque se mostró contrario a una reconversión "salvaje". El presidente del comité de empresa de Hijos de J. Barreras, José Iglesias, afirmó que la privatización de este astillero, que como prevé el INI, tendría dramatiza como efecto.

Los trabajadores de Astilleros Españoles en Sestao daran su visto bueno hoy durante dos horas para asistir a una asamblea. De proseguir el Plan, la planta fin de 2.456 empleados pasará a ser de 1.090 en esta factoría.

Hunosa deja la diversificación en flores y tomates por presiones

ASAJA acusa a Hunosa hacerle competencia desleal al tratar de enderezar el rumbo de la empresa estatal minera a base de adentrarse en el campo de la agricultura y la ganadería utilizando dinero público.

Madrid.—Hunosa ha decidido vender la participación que posee del 32,5% en la sociedad Hortalizas y Plantas (HORTPLASA), que se dedica en la localidad de Mieres a la gestión de invernaderos en los que se producían tomates y plantas ornamentales.

La empresa estatal mineral ha tomado este acuerdo ante las presiones y acciones de protesta que lleva a cabo desde hace unos días la Asociación Agraria de Jóvenes Agricultores (ASAJA).

La sociedad tenía previsto producir anualmente 200.000 plantas ornamentales y 350.000 kilos de tomates y formaba parte de los proyectos de diversificación de las cuencas mineras asturianas, iniciada en una parte por Hunosa.

Su capital social asciende a 4 millones de pesetas y la inversión que se realizó en los invernaderos alcanzó a 128 millones de pesetas.

Hunosa posee el 32,5% de las acciones de esta sociedad mientras que el 67,5% restante está en manos de la iniciativa privada entre ellas Central Agroalimentaria de Productos Asturianos, la Cooperativa de ganaderos de Gijón, Asociación Agrícola, la firma San Agustín, la firma Soto y Rozándara.

La empresa nacional minera vendrá el asociaciones agropecuarias de la sociedad agrícola.

Le Soleil
Québec, Canada

"Otra cosa es que todos ellos (los periódicos) parecen esforzarse en ayudar a los lectores. Muchos trabajos se concentran en las historias, en trozos de información que pueden asimilarse. En una sociedad cuyo tiempo se encuentra altamente restringido, estos periódicos se esfuerzan mucho más por conservar el interés de sus lectores," dijo Peter Bhatia, administrador gerente de The Oregonian, de Portland, Oregon.

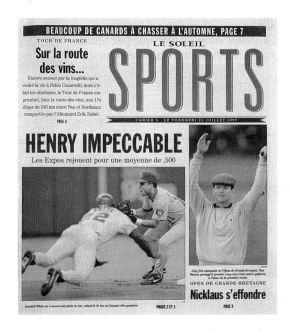

SPECTACLES Arts

Une femme heureuse
Han Suyin ne cesse de surprendre

MAGAZINE DIMANCHE

Ouf! Quel Festival!

Moments magiques

wem
week-end magazine
Le vendredi 21 juillet 1995

Fouiner rue Saint-Jean
Un trajet idéal pour les amateurs de magasins de disques et de livres d'occasion

DOSSIERS

ORIGINE DES BANDES DE MOTARDS CRIMINALISÉS

Des anciens combattants incapables de vivre en paix

Des signes et symboles révélateurs
Les ailes, crânes et nombres qui ornent les vestes ou le corps ne sont pas que «décoratifs»

Reforma

México City, Mexico

Local content was a big factor for the World's Best.

"People want to pick up their local paper and have it feel like their local paper," said Sue Dean, editor and vice president, The Sun News, Myrtle Beach, S.C. "The small papers are a little more adept at local coverage because that's what they do all the time, but the big papers chosen here also have come on strong with local news. Local readers demand local news."

San Francisco Examiner
San Francisco, CA

El contenido local fue un factor importante para los mejores del mundo.

"La gente quiere tomar su periódico local y sentir que es su periódico local," dijo Sue Dean, editora y vicepresidenta de The Sun News, de Myrtle Beach, Carolina del Sur. "Los periódicos pequeños se dedican un poco más a la cobertura local, porque es lo que hacen siempre. Pero los periódicos grandes escogidos aquí, también conceden una gran importancia a las noticias locales. Los lectores locales exigen noticias locales."

The Scotsman

Edinburgh, Scotland

After three days of going through newspaper after newspaper, the judges were able to pinpoint some general trends:

Use of photographs. "The papers that were not selected often made indiscriminately large use of photographs; I guess in the belief that a large photo will automatically make an impact," said Bob Giles, editor and publisher, The Detroit (Mich.) News. "The photos that make the impact are the sharpest images, the most dramatic visuals — not simply the largest."

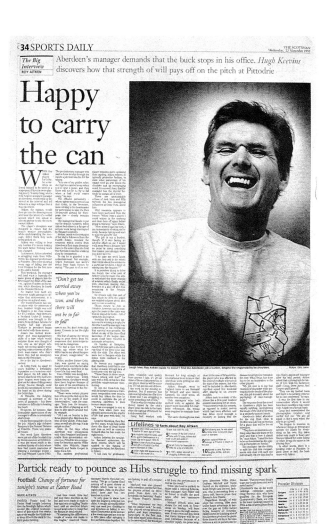

The Big Interview — ROY AITKEN

Aberdeen's manager demands that the buck stops in his office. *Hugh Keevins* discovers how that strength of will pays off on the pitch at Pittodrie

Happy to carry the can

"Don't get too carried away when you've won, and then there will not be so far to fall"

Laugh lines: Roy Aitken insists he doesn't fear the Aberdeen job a burden, despite the responsibility he shoulders.

Partick ready to pounce as Hibs struggle to find missing spark

Football: *Change of fortunes for tonight's teams at Easter Road*

MIKE AITKEN

THE ROSEMARY WEST TRIAL

Murdered by her mother and father, and buried in the garden at Cromwell Street — Heather West

The first and youngest victim, who suffered intolerably at the hands of Rosemary West — Charmaine West

Murdered when she was eight-months pregnant with Fred West's child — Shirley Anne Robinson

The doomed daughter

Heather West: *Her tragedy sparked the inquiry that proved her parents' undoing*

NIC OUTTERSIDE

Charmaine West

Wilful child who became Rosemary's first victim

MARTIN HANNAN

John McLachlan wonders to this day if there are more victims of Fred West buried in the centre of Glasgow

Shirley Anne Robinson

Lonely girl who fell under 'spell'

LYNN COCHRANE

Bruises that linger on 30 years later

The Glasgow years: Three decades on, an ex-lover remembers one of the victims

SARAH WILSON

Hole by hole guide

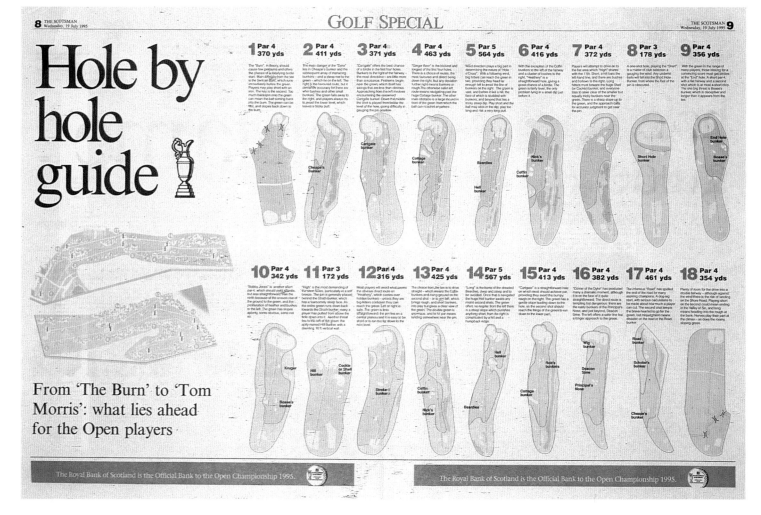

From 'The Burn' to 'Tom Morris': what lies ahead for the Open players

| 1 Par 4 370 yds | 2 Par 4 411 yds | 3 Par 4 371 yds | 4 Par 4 463 yds | 5 Par 5 564 yds | 6 Par 4 416 yds | 7 Par 4 372 yds | 8 Par 3 178 yds | 9 Par 4 356 yds |

| 10 Par 4 342 yds | 11 Par 3 172 yds | 12 Par 4 316 yds | 13 Par 4 425 yds | 14 Par 5 567 yds | 15 Par 4 413 yds | 16 Par 4 382 yds | 17 Par 4 461 yds | 18 Par 4 354 yds |

The Spokesman-Review
Spokane, WA

Después de examinar los periódicos uno a uno durante tres días, los jueces pudieron indicar algunas tendencias generales:

La utilización de fotografías. "Los periódicos que no fueron escogidos, a menudo hicieron un uso indiscriminado y extenso de las fotografías, convencidos, según creo, de que una gran foto causa automáticamente una gran impresión," dijo Bob Giles, editor y director de The Detroit News, de Michigan. "Las fotos que dejan huellas son las de imágenes más nítidas y composición más impresionante, no simplemente las mayores."

OUTDOORS & TRAVEL

SECTION G
Sunday, July 16, 1995
The Spokesman-Review
Spokane, Wash./Coeur d'Alene, Idaho

Inside
Getaway/G2
Travel/G4

'Tread Lightly' when traveling off beaten path

Forest Service pledge urges responsible use of 4-wheelers

Cutthroat evolved with a taste for insects, and a weakness for dry flies. Among trout they are particularly susceptible to fishing pressure and habitat changes.

A cutt above the rest

By Charlie Powell

Cuttroat silently slipping out of sight

By Ben Long

Out & About

Hills alive with beargrass pickers

South American weed migrates to NW lakes

The plant has tiny spines on its leaflet edges and small white flowers that bloom in mid- to late summer.

Sunday
SPORTS

Just when Seattle looked like a baseball town, says John Blanchette, the bigness

Economic showers leave M's without Tino and Blowers

By Dan Weaver

Weary Rockets trip up Chiefs

WSU's Isaac Fontaine (22), Terrance Mack being rebound as Jason Cipollo (30), Syracuse close in on 77-70 win.

Cougars fall short at buzzer

Orangemen win Carrier Classic, surviving Antrim's last-second try

By Steve Bergum

Scoreboard

George wins Heisman in a rout

Page A13
Sunday, July 16, 1995
The Spokesman-Review
Spokane, Wash./Coeur d'Alene, Idaho

Educate trustees
See Page A15

PERSPECTIVE

Readers speak their minds on property rights initiative

Give and takings

Expo's star shines bright and green

By Chris Peck

SECTION B
Sunday, July 16, 1995
The Spokesman-Review
Spokane, Wash./Coeur d'Alene, Idaho

Three killed, three critically injured in car accident/B3

Stand down
Funerals/B4

THE REGION

Internet users resisting critics' slap

Ties to pornography, extremists largely hype, network defenders say

By Tom Sowa

Joining the conversation

Shelly Morgan

Pie from the sky

Senseless act clouds teen's bright future

By Doug Clark

New law sought after girl's death

Group wants sex offenders put in jail right after conviction

By Rachel Konrad

Keeping the pulse

Drumming, dancing classes get students into a rhythm

By Brian Coddington

In hubcap heaven

Chrome domes, spinners and wire hubcaps treated as art as well as business

The State
Columbia, SC

Synergy of visuals. "More thought is going into the display of graphic elements," said Toni Piqué, consultant for Innovación Periodística and former section editor at La Vanguardia, Barcelona, Spain. "Both photos and information graphics have been scaled back and are now being used to complement each other while more effectively telling the story. Photographers don't win, artists don't win...but the reader wins."

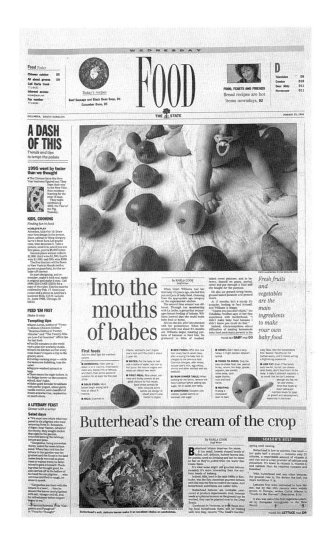

Diario de Noticias
Huarte-Pamplona, Spain

La sinergia de los componentes visuales. "El despliegue de los elementos gráficos obedece a una mayor reflexión," dijo Toni Piqué, asesor de innovación periodística y antiguo editor de sección de La Vanguardia, de Barcelona, España. "Tanto las fotos como las gráficas informativas han disminuido, y se utilizan actualmente como complementos mutuos, mientras se narra la historia con mayor eficacia. Los fotógrafos y los artistas no ganan... pero el lector sí."

AYUNTAMIENTO Constituida con buenas perspectivas la Mesa del Casco Antiguo — 22

EDUCACIÓN El Consejo Social de la UPNA aprueba un presupuesto de 5.004 millones — 25

Fallece calcinado en un choque frontal en Puente la Reina

Dos personas más resultaron heridas graves

INCENDIO Vista de dos de los coches accidentados tras el incendio.

HERIDO Los equipos rescatan a Ángel Barea, gravemente herida.

MOTOR Uno de ellos salió desplazado cien metros.

D.N. Pamplona

Una persona resultó muerta y dos heridas de gravedad tras un accidente de tráfico ocurrido ayer en las cercanías de Puente la Reina. La colisión frontal de dos de los tres vehículos implicados provocó un incendio del que no pudo escapar el fallecido, quien murió calcinado.

GRAVES

Las unidades de rescate desplazadas a Puente la Reina tuvieron que desarmar el vehículo para sacar al herido más grave, Ángel Barrio Salvador.

Diario de **Noticias** EDITORIAL

DEJE SU MENSAJE

☎ 330017

No se publicarán aquellas llamadas en las que el comunicante no se identifique.

Guardería de Mendebaldea

Felicidades, Amaia

Casco Antiguo

El día del juez

EL JUEZ DE INSTRUCCIÓN Nº 1 DE PAMPLONA, JUAN Manuel Fernández, dio ayer un importante paso en la investigación de la llamada trama navarra del caso Roldán.

Día Mundial del SIDA

¡NO, GRACIAS! DE ESO ANDO SOBRAO

SENTENCIAS

Navarra ha guardado su identidad a lo largo de siglos

Javier Otano
Pte. de Navarra

CIFRA DEL DÍA

6.000

PERSONAJES DEL DÍA

LOLA EGUREN
Pta. del Parlamento

ANTONIO ARAGÓN
Consejero

MIGUEL Á. ANCÍZAR
Sindicalista

MESA DE REDACCIÓN

¿De qué se ríe?

Manuel Beza

SOS NAVARRA

088

POLICÍA FORAL · BOMBEROS · AMBULANCIAS

FARMACIAS DE GUARDIA

Tel. 222111-227718

PAMPLONA, DE 9 A 22 HORAS

DE 22 A 9 HORAS

LA SUERTE

PRIMITIVA

1 19 31
32 36 43

Sábado, 30 de diciembre

COMPLEMENTARIO 42 REINTEGRO 1

ONCE

57.798

CUPONAZO: SERIE 233

Cielos muy nubosos y nieve sobre los 1.500 metros

PASAJEROS

AUTOBUSES

TRENES

AVIONES

TELÉFONOS

Verano'95

REGRESO

Raphael se instala con su familia en España

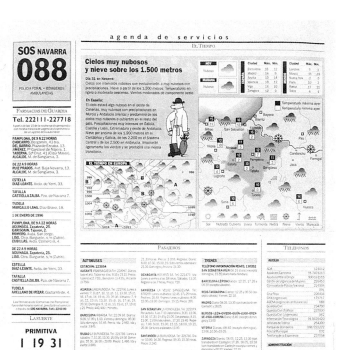

LIZ HURLEY LE PERDONA La novia de Hugh Grant le perdona su desliz.

VIAJE DE NOVIOS

Paola Dominguín y Manuel Villalta celebran su luna de miel en Cádiz

Chabeli piensa ya en la maternidad al lado de Carlos, su nuevo amor

"Es un hombre muy seguro que me quiere muchísimo"

NIEVES SALINAS CORPRESS

EN ESPAÑA Chabeli Iglesias y Carlos Trápaga ya están en Madrid.

BURBUJAS

Marlon Brando vuelve al cine con 'Divine rapture'

El asesino Manson graba y edita un disco desde la cárcel

La mujer de Sergio Dalma, Maribel Sanz, dará a luz en agosto

El segundo hijo de Paquirri quiere estudiar empresariales y marketing en Madrid

Paloma Picasso se divorcia de Rafael López-Cambil

¿QUIÉN ES ÉL?

El Observador
Montevideo, Uruguay

Quality control. "I was stunned by seeing many newspapers where the quality of printing and reproduction is very, very poor," said Bob Giles, editor and publisher, The Detroit (Mich.) News. "This should be handled internally by paying attention to quality and setting standards. It can make an enormous difference in how the paper looks, and how the community feels about its paper."

Brasil pretende revisar las excepciones al comercio intraMercosur
· Página 10

La inflación europea muestra desparejos comportamientos
· Página 11

■ FINANCIAMIENTO

Desregularán los créditos hipotecarios

La iniciativa apunta a dinamizar el sector de la construcción y posibilitar un mayor acceso de la población a la vivienda propia

El Ministerio de Economía y Finanzas (MEF) estudia impulsar un proyecto de ley para autorizar a los bancos privados a conceder préstamos hipotecarios sobre edificios sin terminar, lo que establecería una importante modificación en la regulación del sector financiero y posibilitaría que la industria de la construcción retome su dinamismo en seis u ocho meses, confiaron a *El Observador* fuentes oficiales y privadas.

El proyecto que ya fue redactado y está en la etapa de consultas, se originó en una iniciativa de la Asociación de Promotores Privados de la Construcción (APPC).

El planteo de la gremial apuntó a dar respuesta tanto a la necesidad de aumentar la oferta de vivienda, sobre todo en rubros accesibles para amplios sectores populares, como a la de recuperar los niveles de empleo, los que han disminuido como consecuencia de la tendencia recesiva que domina al sector.

Hasta el momento, sólo el Banco Hipotecario del Uruguay (BHU) está legalmente habilitado a realizar financiamientos sobre la garantía de edificios en construcción, explican las fuentes.

De transformarse en ley, el proyecto eliminaría el monopolio del BHU en esta área y, los bancos privados podrán volcar recursos para desarrollar líneas de financiamiento en esa dirección.

> Hasta el momento sólo el BHU está legalmente habilitado a hipotecar edificios en construcción

La Asociación de Bancos del Uruguay (ABU), consultada por *El Observador* sobre la iniciativa, manifestó su acuerdo "con la idea básica" y expresó algunas "sugerencias" para ajustar la redacción del proyecto de ley.

Por otra parte, los informantes señalaron que si bien el proyecto de ley y los estímulos complementarios a definir son un asunto que está en la órbita del MEF, el...

Banco Central tiene conocimiento de la propuesta y en términos generales "no tiene reparo" sobre ésta.

Fuentes participantes de las tratativas indicaron a *El Observador* que la desmonopolización del BHU genera posibilidades muy amplias tanto en el sector financiero como para la industria de la construcción.

El MEF estudia aprobar estímulos adicionales a las empresas del sector construcción que están dispuestas a aumentar la oferta de...

Mosca respalda la iniciativa P. BIELLI

■ MERCOSUR

Ahora Brasil quiere revisar las listas de adecuación

Pretende reabrir la negociación de las excepciones internas

Las desavenencias entre musulmanes de Zepa amenazan con utilizar como escudos humanos...

[texto continúa]

Indicadores

DOLAR — El dólar cerró a 6 milésimas del piso en mercado ofrecido

ACCIONES — Fanapel subió 3,45% tras estar pedidas durante varios días

BOLSA NY — Wall Street frenó la tendencia alcista con un retroceso de 0,39%

DOLAR NY — El dólar se recuperó por alentadores datos económicos en EEUU

BOLSA BS AS — Merval avanzó 1,7% impulsado por acciones telefónicas

La Izquierda Unida implica directamente a González por caso GAL
· Página 27

■ MUSULMANES AMENAZAN USAR CASCOS AZULES COMO ESCUDOS HUMANOS

ONU ante una situación límite en Bosnia

Enfrenta la peor encrucijada desde el inicio de la guerra: si la OTAN ataca, los serbios bombardearán Zepa y, si no lo hace, efectivos de ONU serán utilizados de escudos humanos

Sarajevo también bajo fuego. Un soldado intenta salvar a un bebé de los morteros serbios

LA CUENTA REGRESIVA PARA ZEPA

Tropas serbio-bosnias apoyadas por tanques están a 500 metros del centro de Zepa, enclave musulmán ubicado al este de Bosnia, según informaron fuentes de ONU

Los defensores del enclave musulmán de Zepa amenazaron ayer con utilizar como escudos humanos a los 79 cascos azules ucranianos que se encuentran en la zona si la aviación de la OTAN no ataca a las fuerzas serbiobosnias que rodean la ciudad.

Por su parte, los serbiobosnios también han amenazado con...

> Los bosnios arrebataron equipos, armas y vehículos a los cascos azules

CAOS TAMBIÉN EN GORAZDE

El Ejército bosnio en Gorazde, enclave oriental bosnio amparado por la ONU, se ha apoderado de la mayor parte de las armas y municiones de los cascos azules ucranianos desplegados en la zona, indicó ayer el portavoz en Zagreb.

> Los niños de la guerra

Un 60% de los cerca de 30 mil refugiados en Bosnia, desde el conflicto del enclave de Srebrenica son niños, informó ayer Marie Heuze, portavoz del Fondo de Naciones Unidas para la Infancia (Unicef).

Se cumplen 10 años de Live Aid, el concierto más importante de rock
· Página 18

CRÍTICA CD · A SPANNER IN THE WORKS

Rod Stewart le sigue pegando fuerte

El cantante escocés ha regresado con un disco cargado de espontaneidad y canciones vibrantes que explican por qué lleva más de 25 años de carrera signados por el éxito

POR ALEJANDRO ESPINA
de la redacción de EL OBSERVADOR

A SPANNER IN THE WORKS

Artista: Rod Stewart
Sello: Warner Bros.
Temas: Windy Town, The Downtown Lights, Leave Virginia Alone, Sweetheart Like You, This Lady Luck, You're The Star, Muddy, Sam And Otis, Hang On St. Christopher, Delicious, Soothe Me, Purple Heather.
Calificación: (****) Muy Bueno

> La selección de autores tan diversos es el principal sostén del disco

---

Damon Hill logró el primer lugar en el circuito de Silverstone
· Página 31

Gonzalo Rodríguez larga octavo hoy en la Fórmula 3 Británica
· Página 31

TOUR DE FRANCIA · JALABERT SUBIÓ AL TERCER LUGAR

Un galo dividió a los españoles

El francés Laurent Jalabert del equipo Once ganó la duodécima etapa del Tour de Francia y acortó diferencias con el líder Miguel Induráin

Hubo guerra entre equipos españoles en esta etapa, un galo del equipo Once ganó...

Festejo a lo grande REUTER

LAS FRASES

L. Jalabert

■ "Hemos tratado de derrumbar el trono de Induráin, pero se ha mostrado sólido y firme como una roca"

■ "Hay que estar atento. Quién sabe lo que puede ocurrir. Hoy el equipo de Induráin la pasó mal durante muchos kilómetros"

■ "Me estoy volviendo ambicioso y aspiro a todo"

> Jalabert llegó a sacar una ventaja de once minutos al líder Miguel Induráin

CLASIFICACIÓN GRAL.

1º M. Induráin (Esp)	52h46m05s	
2º Alex Zulle (Sui)	a 2m44s	
3º Bjarne Riis (Din)	a 6m00s	
4º Melchor Mauri (Esp)	a 7m49s	
5º Tony Rominger (Sui)	a 9m47s	
6º Ivan Gotti (Ita)	a 11m48s	
7º Marco Pantani (Ita)	a 12m36s	
8º Fernando Escartín (Esp)	a 14m20s	
9º Claudio Chiappucci (Ita)	a 14m26s	

> El español reaccionó y acortó la diferencia horaria apoyado en el trabajo de Banesto

The Home News
East Brunswick, NJ

El control de calidad. "Me asombró ver muchos periódicos de una pésima calidad en la edición y la reproducción," dijo Bob Giles, redactor e editor de The Detroit News (Michigan). "Esto debería resolverse a nivel interno, prestando atención a la calidad y estableciendo normas. Esto puede hacer que la apariencia del periódico y la acogida que le dé su comunidad, sean muy diferentes."

SATURDAY
MAY 6, 1995

THE Dēsign
SECTION
of THE HOME NEWS

"No house should ever be on any hill or on anything. It should be of the hill, belonging to it, so hill and house could live together each the happier for the other."
— FRANK LLOYD WRIGHT in 1957

INSIDE: Lamps, Auction racks with heat of Collectibles, D3

THE

By MARY PRICE · Home News Design section editor

Psssst. Wallpaper has a checkered past.
It wasn't always the hip and versatile surface material seen today.
Once it was drab. Uninspired. Old-fashioned. And going nowhere.
Wallpaper was on its way out when post-war Americans headed en masse to the 'burbs, with visions of lawn mowers and carports dancing in their heads. The suburban utopias awaited. Ah, the good life.
The cookie-cutter tract houses of the 1950s were easy on monthly payments ($58) but high on BORING. The pioneers of the suburbs were turned off with the status quo and were turned on to the decorating miracle du jour — pre-mixed latex paint.
Wallpaper manufacturers, faced with rapidly declining sales, needed to juice things up.
They introduced do-it-yourself wallpaper and

PAPER

WAYS TO HANG IT: All you ever wanted to know about papering — cost, cutting, pasting and how to cut corners (literally).
Graphic, D3

gave their designers free rein. Katzenbach and Warren even commissioned artists, such as Henri Matisse, Joan Miro and Alexander Calder. Their work on wallpaper can be seen at an exhibit at New York's Cooper-Hewitt Museum.
Now suburbanites had choices — would it be California villas, outdoor vistas, doves, flowers or buttons they pasted on the walls?
But wait. Designs only got wilder.
The fusion of abstract imagery and everyday objects produced some of the most bizarre wallpaper designs of the 1950s — boomerangs and amoeba shapes, doodles and drips.
Joanne Warner, Cooper-Hewitt's wallcoverings curator, sees wallpaper as more than home furnishing, more than simple decoration. "Like archaeological discoveries, wallpaper reveals much about the life and times of the age in which it was created."
— *Peter Genovese contributed to this story*

ROUTE

UNDER $50
Excellent objects for you & your dwelling

Warning: Curves ahead
This austere metal vase caught my eye right away. You can sneak fresh flowers (it's LED-light) or dry twigs. But with this figure it looks great sans the trimming.
Spotted at: Holly-wood, 'n vinre — 101 Albany St. Kilmer Square, New Brunswick (908) 828-2800. Ask for Bernie or Marie.
Price: $37

STRUCTURE
A second glance at local architecture

Architect: Robert C. Venturi
Background: Born in Philadelphia, 1925. A graduate of Princeton University and the American Academy, Rome. Author of "Complexity and Contradiction in Architecture." Some call it the most important writing on architecture since Le Corbusier's "Vers une Architecture."
Building: Gordon Wu Hall, Butler College cafeteria, 1983.
Where: Elm Drive, Princeton University. View of Wu Hall's dining room bay window, with limestone insets floating above.
Sources: "Contemporary Architects," published by St. James Press and "Pride of Place: Building the American Dream" by Robert A.M. Stern.

GARDEN MARKET
Cool products & stuff fresh from the garden

Snip it in the bud
For delicate stemming, shaping or thinning jobs in the garden, floral snips by Fiskars do the job and for little money ($4.99). Intense warranty, available at Caldor).
Features:
1 Finger loop for greater control
2 Stainless steel blades.
3 Lightweight construction.
4 Fits comfortably in your hand.

See RILEY, page B2

INSIDE
Gallup Poll examines religious preferences of Americans · B3
RELIGION CALENDAR · B3
CHURCH DIRECTORY · B3
CLASSIFIED · B4

INSPIRATIONS
The Rev. Joan Fleming, Christ Church of the City of New Brunswick, 5 Paterson St., cites the book "Gravity and Grace" by Simone Weil. Weil explains that just as gravity attracts by equal force, so do we react equal emotion. But grace intervenes to help us react with equal dignity, Flemming says.

RELIGION & ETHICS

B SECTION
SATURDAY
May 6, 1995

Michael Riley · *Only Human*

Cleaning house — and heart

Once we got past the problem with the "Edgerods" and the gas-smuggling incident, things went pretty smooth with Mum's move into the nursing home.

[body text continues]

The three gravestones at the center of this photograph mark the site of remains that will be moved for the construction of a walkway at the First Reformed Church of New Brunswick. The walkway, which will be covered, will ease access between the church house and the church.

MAKING WAY FOR THE LIVING

By SHARON SEITZ
Home News Staff Writer

R.I.P. Requiescat in Pace. Rest in Peace.
However it's written, that familiar phrase often appears on tombstones, offering comforting reassurance that a departed loved one's final resting place will remain forever undisturbed.

"I don't want to say it's an everyday occurrence, but there's nothing that is inherently shocking about it. . . Disinterments are not that unusual."
— WILLIAM B. WAITS
Executive director, N.J. Cemetery Board

See GRAVES, page B2

PLACES OF WORSHIP: Ahavas Achim Congregation

Address and phone: 216 First Ave., Highland Park, (908) 247-0532
Spiritual leader: Rabbi Ronald Schwartzberg
History: The Orthodox Jewish Ahavas Achim Congregation was established in 1889 in New Brunswick...

Compiled by Karen Fisk; Photograph by Dick Costello/The Home News

---

TRAVEL
SECTION I
SUNDAY
July 16, 1995

TIP
Nationwide beacon: The U.S. Lighthouse Society, a nonprofit organization based in San Francisco, promotes restoration and preservation of the county's more than 850 lighthouses and publishes a quarterly magazine. To join, write to 244 Kearny St., fifth floor, San Francisco, Calif, 94108. Membership dues are $25.

Trip of the Week
Mild to wild

Passport
Music in the air
Classical festivals are in bloom throughout the nation.

Update
Reality check
There's a gap between consumers' travel concerns and government action.

Life
in the past lane

At the Norlands Living History Center in Maine, you can experience 19th-century farm life for a weekend.

Story by Patrick Soran Correspondent

The renovated Congregational Church (left), near Livermore, Maine, is the centerpiece of Norlands Living History Center. Participants (right) practice penmanship with quill pens.

See PAST, page F7

Detroit turning the beat around

By LOIS FEGAN
Home News Correspondent

Detroit's Greektown glitters at night. It's a popular spot for those looking for good food and lively nightspots.

See DETROIT, page F4

ENTERTAINMENT
H SECTION
SUNDAY
May 7, 1995

It's worth spending a day in the big city to see actress Helen Mirren star in Ivan Turgenev's "A Month in the Country" at New York's Roundabout Theatre. F. Murray Abraham co-stars in the 1872 play.

THEATER PAGE 2

"Dr. Zhivago" is rejuvenated for its 30th anniversary, and actor Omar Sharif reminisces about his role in the tale of ill-fated love.

MOVIES PAGE 3

To understand John Paul II the Pope, one must strive to understand Karol Jozef Wojtyla the man, says Tad Szulc, author of "John Paul II: The Biography."

BOOKS PAGE 8

NEIL SEDAKA
★ ★ ★

The tra-la days aren't over

The man on the other end of the telephone has a voice so polite, so measured, you feel you ought to call him Mr. Sedaka.
"Good morning. How are you?"
Warm, resonant, and perfectly on pitch, this voice belongs to the composer and singer whose career has spanned 13 Top 10 hits, spanned four decades, and, recently, scored a star on the Hollywood Walk of Fame.

includes a date Saturday at the State Theatre, New Brunswick.

CHAPTER I
Sedaka, son of a New York cab driver, grew up in the Brighton Beach section of Brooklyn. Music was in his genes: His grandmother was a concert pianist.

Story by Andrea Feld, Home News Correspondent · Illustration by Tom Kerr, The Home News

See SEDAKA, page H5

INSIDE: It's Fair Time! For a complete schedule of events, see Stepping Out.

Jackson Hole News

Jackson, Wyoming — Wednesday, July 26, 1995 — 50 cents

Parents want cease-fire in day care war

■ Nasty dispute splits board, staff at Community Children's Project.

By Mark Huffman

Parents of kids enrolled in the valley's largest day care program told battling administrators and board members last night to go to a neutral corner and seek professional mediation.

During a two-hour meeting, parents were dismayed that the board and staff of the Community Children's Project have fought to a standstill over who has power to make decisions for the program.

The conflict between elected and hired leaders of CCP included board allegations of poor administration and failures in taking care of children.

But a fight over who is responsible for what was the center of the storm.

Board member Chris Thulin said the board and staff had "come to an impasse about the best way to handle problems," and that CCP administrator Carol Brodie had ignored the legal orders of the board. Brodie, who called two weeks ago for the board to resign, said the board had held "secret meetings" and issued "inappropriate directions" she felt compelled to disobey.

Thulin and the only two other members remaining on the diminished board — Christie Knori and Jan Woodmencey — said they would give up the posts they were elected to in January if parents demanded it but wouldn't quit because staff wanted them gone.

"We work for you, the parents, and it is not up to the administration to demand we resign," Thulin said. Knori told the audience that "if you want our resignation, we're here to resign to you, the parents, not the administration."

Continued on page 23A

▸ BUCKIN' BUSKIN

Buskin Wilson blasts out of the chute on his short-go bull to win second in the round and fifth in the nation during the National High School Finals Rodeo in Gillette Sunday. See Sports for coverage of Jackson Hole rodeo competitors at the week-long event.

Workers still here despite camp ban

■ Forest crackdown doesn't create feared shock waves.

By Roger Hayden

A policy banning long-term camping in national forests around Jackson hasn't caused a shortage of seasonal employees, illegal camping on private lands or other feared effects.

"Any of the dire predictions we had are just not happening at all," said Dan Bauer, the Bridger-Teton National Forest's chief law enforcement officer. "Whatever we did prior to getting out in the woods worked really well."

Forest officials imposed the policy before the usual 300 to 1,000 seasonal employees came to Jackson to camp in the Bridger-Teton National Forest. They set a two-to-five-day limit to prevent damage and increasingly unsanitary conditions.

Other districts of the Bridger-Teton allow recreational camping up to 16 days in one location.

Bauer thinks campers realized they would have to compete for scarce and expensive housing in Jackson or stay away.

"We just didn't find the numbers that have been historically out there," Bauer said.

He and two other temporary officers from forests in California patrol the Bridger-Teton on motorcycles and on foot. Since mid-May, they've contacted 200 campers and cited six.

Bauer and his crew make the rounds of traditional workers' camping spots such

Continued on page 23A

Park may be Clinton soapbox

■ President has a chance to score with voters while on vacation in Jackson Hole.

By Angus M. Thuermer Jr.

President Clinton has an opportunity to score political points while on vacation in Jackson Hole by highlighting support for the environment, conservationists say.

Although the president has not used his vacations in the past to issue any proclamations, this summer might be different. Vacationing near and in Grand Teton National Park, Clinton could focus on the differences between himself and the GOP-controlled Congress, which has been on a rampage against environmental laws.

THE FIRST FAMILY'S VISIT TO JACKSON HOLE

National Park Service officials hope the president will do more than just play — that he will use the Tetons as a backdrop for a message about federal lands and their value.

"The Park Service is looking for an appropriate event, if the president will take the time out of his vacation to do that," Park Service spokesman David Barna in Washington said.

Clinton is expected to vacation in Jackson Hole the last two weeks of August. That would put him here on Aug. 25, National Park Founders' Day. Founders' Day is the day the Park Service commemorates the system of national parks, which began with establishment of the world's first National Park — Yellowstone — in 1872. Founders' Day is celebrated annually by waiving park

Continued on page 23A

C Cache Creek run – 3C · Below the Rim – 4C · Sports Briefs – 7C · Sports Review – 9C

SPORTS

BUSINESS NEWS *See page 11C* · CLASSIFIED ADS *See page 14C*

Jackson Hole News — Wednesday, July 19, 1995

OUTDOORS
PAUL BRUUN

Dealing with dirty rivers

You could have knocked Fred Staehr over with a feather several years ago when he drove up to a rather soiled Madison River.

The veteran Jackson school teacher and fishing guide was helping some other Montana guides with a fly-fishing clinic and was stunned when everyone else happily began rigging to fish.

"You can't catch trout in water like this," Fred whispered to one of his counterparts as he gawked at what would generally be referred to a *stained* water.

"Sure we can, Fred," assured the guide. "Remember, this is the Madison, and we're fishing for browns and rainbows. They'll hit nymphs like crazy in this water."

"I didn't believe it," Fred later explained to me, "but they were right. The fish climbed all over both large and small nymphs. If that had been here in Jackson, we wouldn't have caught a thing."

And that, frustrated reader, is the rest of the story about catching fish on artificials in Jackson Hole when the water is off-color. Lately

Continued on page 10C

Big buckles, little riders

■ Cowboys and cowgirls hit the fences and the dirt in the Little Buckaroo Rodeo.

By Thomas Dewell

Travis Wyss and Cal Walker were set to duel like cowboys of yore.

Both scored a 63 in the first go of the 7- to 9-year-old bareback riding competition at the 60-rider Little Buckaroo Rodeo at the Jackson rodeo grounds Sunday. To break the tie, the judges called for a ride-off. The winner would take a shiny silver buckle home.

Walker climbed into the chute and aboard a white pony, a descendant of the Shetlands that were used in old Kemmerer coal mines. When the iron crashed open, the horse sped around the ring like demon, running at full tilt.

The rodeo clown chased Walker down and lifted him from the pony. Although the horse didn't buck, the judges awarded a 60.

Ornery critter ready to deliver

Wyss, in his first-ever Buckaroo rodeo, knew he needed a good ride to win. His Shetland had been stomping in the chute; the ornery critter was ready to deliver.

As Wyss burst into the arena, the pony kicked high and bucked like a rodeo pro. Wyss held on with both hands as the pony dodged the clown and headed for the fence.

Wyss was dumped into the green rails, banging his head against the metal. He lay in the arena dirt quietly, then shook his head before he climbed to his feet. The judges awarded the ride a 70, and Wyss won the buckle.

"I'm proud of myself," the 9-year-old said, "and still a little hurty."

Cowboy battles tough cow

Although Walker missed the bareback buckle, he did win the 7- to 9-year-old calf riding. The cowboy battled a tough little cow that ran toward the fence before

Continued on page 7C

Jake Greenwood, 12, of Big Piney, catches some rare air during the bronc busting in the Little Buckaroo Rodeo Sunday.

New world speed record is set in Town Square

■ Kerry Schlager breaks 99 white pine boards in 14.765 seconds.

By Thomas Dewell

They say records were made to be broken. In Kerry Schlager's case, boards and records were made to be broken.

Using his Taekwondo hand chop, Schlager snapped 99 white pine boards in 14.765 seconds in the Town Square Saturday. The boards, stacked in threes, were set along a 40-foot stretch of the boardwalk.

With a shuffle step Schlager moved down the row and hacked each stack with bare hand. Each pop sounded like the blast of a shotgun.

"I was going with everything I had," Schlager said. "I stayed focused and gave everything I had.

Terry Schlager swings on his last boards Saturday as he sets a world record for board breaking.

If you don't, you only break one or two of them."

Schlager's instructor, Mark Cress, stood behind him, hollering encouragement as the crowd roared. The third-degree black belt bested the old world speed record — 19.76 seconds— by nearly five clicks.

> *"I was going with everything I had."*
> — *Kerry Schlager*, RECORD BOARD BREAKER

Two years ago, Schlager tried to break 299 boards in one minute but cracked only 295 pieces of timber. He fell short of the record because the snapped boards were falling back toward his feet, making him stumbles as he moved between board-breaking stations. This time Cress and Schlager lined the stations in a row so Schlager wouldn't trip.

Schlager, 43, works on the Moulton Ranch and does everything from fixing fences to repairing equipment. Taekwondo has been a way for him "to keep out of trouble."

In Taekwondo, athletes break boards during some tests. To receive a purple belt, a participant must snap a single board with a leg kick and show proficiency in forms, sparring combinations and self defense.

After Schlager's record-setting performance, tourists and onlookers quickly gathered up the broken pine and had Schlager sign the leftovers of his world record. His hand trembled at first as adrenaline continued to surge through his system.

"The adrenaline, it was just unreal," Schlager said.

Jackson Hole News
Jackson, WY

Use of color. "We need to ensure that color is used more naturally," said Peter Bhatia, managing editor, The Oregonian, Portland, Ore. "It needs to be part of the paper's basic identity, but shouldn't be used just for the sake of using color on a page."

B Sound Bites – 4B · Gardening – 5B · People, Question – 8B · Weddings – 15B

TETON STYLE

Jackson Hole News

Rare birds have been seen here. See Far Afield on page 2B.

Wednesday, July 26, 1995

VIEW *from the* HOLE
MARK HUFFMAN

Read this while you drive down Broadway

You're supposed to pay attention to the road, look straight ahead through the windshield so you avoid running into other cars and people and the miscellaneous items that clutter the surface of the globe and make motoring such a dangerous activity.

But it's hard, what with the distractions. For me, at least. There are so many other things that demand attention when I'm driving: buzzing bees in the car, women on bicycles, interesting birds winging overhead, sale items in shop windows.

Back about 1991 I drove off I-70 because I was intent on seeing my odometer turn 66,666.6, which I had anticipated for weeks, thinking of it as "Satan's mileage." Just before it happened, there was all this loud airhorn honking and I had to swerve around a truck full of nuclear waste or potato chips or something, and I missed seeing all the 6s line up.

Even more years ago, before I stopped, it was cigarettes. I was always trying to find a match or wipe smoky tears from my eyes or snuff a butt or put out a relatively minor car fire at 65 mph.

There was more: I had a bad habit of writing columns while I drove, which resulted in some ugly accidents, a few of which actually made it into print.

But, by the normal process of maturing and concentrating, I left those distractions behind me. I became a better, more attentive driver.

But it all went bad again. In recent years, there's something new to distract me when I drive. It's a question, posed by an observation, an observation forced on me by something the highway people are doing.

Maybe you've observed it too: That the people in charge of the highways seem to have run out of reasons to put up roadside signs — real reasons, that is — and seem to have begun instead to invent reasons. They have

Continued on page 15B

Ah Ah CHOO!

A wet summer produces a pollen plague.

By Roger Hayden

The darkening sky says you'll be running or biking in the rain again today.

Your climb last week was rained out.

And your lawn needs mowing for the second time in a week.

It's been a wet summer, and while that's good for the greenery, it isn't as healthy for many people in the area: If you're among the sensitive ones, you're sneezing, sniffling, rubbing swollen eyes and clearing an itchy throat.

"It's a high pollen count year, and that's because of the moisture," Dr. Bruce Hayse said. Hayse and other

Continued on page 7B

BUSINESS

BUSINESS VIEW
Analysis by Jonathan Schechter

Self-Serve Unleaded Gasoline
Price/Gallon
(chart: 1993-1994 ■ 1994-1995)

THE COST OF A MARKET BASKET of groceries on August 1 fell 29 cents (1 percent) from July 1, totaling $37.05. A year ago, the same market basket of groceries cost $37.79, or 1 percent more than today. This drop comes despite a significant increase in coffee prices versus last year (90 cents per pound, due to last fall's frost in Brazil.)

Note: Since this feature began, Fred's Market has been the source of all prices. Once Fred's closes, Albertsons will become the reference. In this situation, both stores' prices will be examined. This month, Albertsons price for the same 20 items is 8 percent higher than Fred's ($40.02 versus $37.05); last month is was 9.2 percent higher. Of the 20 items, Fred's is cheaper on 11 items, and Albertsons on five.

Additionally, in response to a reader's query, the same calculation was done for the Westside Store. For the same 20 items, prices this month at the Westside Store are 13.2 percent higher than those at Albertsons and a whopping 22.4 percent higher than those at Fred's.

SOURCE: Fred's Market, Albertsons, Westside Store

Market Basket of Groceries
(chart: 93-94 - Fred's ■ 94-95 - Albertson's)

GASOLINE PRICES STAYED flat for the third straight month, with the August 1 price for a gallon of unleaded self-serve gasoline remaining at $1.249. This month's price is 2 cents per gallon (1.6 percent) higher than last August's price.

SOURCE: Various Petroleum

Long-Term Monthly Rental Rates
Price/Bedroom
(chart: 1993-1994 ■ 1994-1995)

THE RENTAL CYCLE PASSED through its semi-annual increase window in May. Supply is high in the two-bedroom rental market, as prices for these units rose barely, if at all. Smaller and larger units rose more, yielding a blended average increase for all units in this survey of 5 percent versus a year ago. The current average rent is $316.57 per bedroom.

SOURCE: Various property managers

Chamber members mull 2% tax

■ Board to decide this month whether to pursue November or February election.

By Angus M. Thuermer Jr.

Members of the Jackson Hole Chamber of Commerce who attended a lodging tax forum last week favor seeking only a 2 percent tax to be voted on in January or February.

A poll of the 30 people attending the session revealed those preferences. A 3 percent tax and a November election date were disfavored.

The vote on the timing of the election was close, however.

Almost as many in attendance favored the November date. Comments from the meeting will be forwarded to the chamber board, which is expected to recommend a course to town and county governments by the end of August.

The 2 percent tax is earmarked for promotion. It failed by 10 percent at the polls last November.

A survey shows that opponents feel that too much of the tax was spent on promotion, not enough on services for visitors.

Chamber director Joe Rogers wouldn't predict that the board would follow the wishes of the small sample.

"I'm not so sure this election is going to be put off," he said of the preference for a winter vote, rather than one in November. "It's going to be up to the board to make the final decision."

Clark Brooks challenged the November timetable.

"It's going to take us five months to put together a campaign," he said. "Even now, we're under the gun to make January. We shouldn't fire with a gun half loaded."

"It takes enormous efforts to get something like this passed," added Bob Graham. "If we don't turn out a lot more than what's in this room, we'll be back in this room a year from now."

Whether the tax should be proposed at only 2 percent also was contested. Eighteen people preferred that level, compared to eight who said the election should be for 3 percent.

"I'm afraid that's the way we're going to have to go," chamber president Jim Sullivan said.

Joe Rogers

campaign.

"Why have the tax for promotion in that case, because there isn't enough," he said.

But the wisdom of seeking a 3 percent tax after the vote for a 2 percent one failed was flailed.

"It takes enormous efforts to get something like this passed. If we don't turn out a lot more than what's in this room, we'll be back in this room a year from now."

— Bob Graham

A 2-percent tax would raise an estimated $1.5 million, compared to $2.3 million if the tax were set at 3 percent.

But $1.5 million might not be enough to promote Jackson Hole adequately and provide visitor services which voters demand. Voters seem committed to funding a START bus system that's cost $400,000 a year in the past, Snow King manager Manuel Lopez said.

If those wishes are followed, there wouldn't be enough for an effective

amenity that separates Jackson Hole from resorts like Vail and Tahoe, one innkeeper said.

There's no possibility the enabling lodging tax legislation will be modified at the upcoming legislative budget session, State Sen. Grant Larson said. A change has been proposed by tax critic Bill Phelps, who would like to see the money given to local and state governments.

Local governments could use the money to provide visitor services, and the state could use its share to advertise Wyoming, Phelps has said. He hasn't received support from legislators.

Today's law requires 90 percent of the funds be used for promotion and "other specific tourism-related objectives." Larson said if Teton County gets to tinkering with the legislation, the state may recognize an opportunity to fund its travel commission with a statewide bed tax, to the county's loss.

Lodging tax proponents had hoped to recommend that the chamber board propose a three percent tax, 50 percent of which would be used for marketing. Twenty percent would be used for the START system, 10 percent on the Town and County for visitor service, 10 percent for visitor information and services and 10 percent for community programs and events.

If such a schedule is adopted, Rogers said, it would amount to a "campaign promise" to spend the money that way. County Commissioner Tom Scheid said it might be possible to commit the proportions on the ballot.

Free busses is a major

Organizations need housing plans

■ Nonprofits that survive may be those that find ways to accommodate employees.

In my last column, I noted that wage increases have not kept pace with housing costs. From that observation, I opined that, within the next few years, this disparity will begin to create significant problems for local organizations.

ECONOMIC PERSPECTIVE
JONATHAN SCHECTER

In particular, I focused on local nonprofits, but the same thought is generally applicable to any local organization which anticipates eventually needing to hire new senior staff/management. If local wages don't meet local housing costs, where

will key employees live?

For the past decade, the general solution to the problem of expensive housing has been for individual employees to make the decision to work in Jackson Hole but live in Idaho (or, increasingly, in Lincoln County). Lord knows how many local businesses feel the pinch when Teton Pass is closed for a day. According to the 1990 census, 30 percent of all working residents of Teton County, Idaho, earned their living in Teton County, Wyo., a number which has surely increased in the last five years.

In many ways, this is not such a bad solution to the problem. Certainly most Jackson Hole residents who "locals" living in Victor or Driggs, and most of my friends living in Idaho feel they have a pretty good

life.

But an interesting phenomenon is occurring, one which suggests to me that, while Idaho may be the solution to much of Jackson Hole's current and future housing needs, it may not work at all well for the type of senior individuals needed to run local nonprofits.

"Quality of life" changes

This phenomenon is simply the aging of the population in Teton County, Idaho. Specifically, it is how this group's thoughts about quality of life are changing as they age. And by "aging of the population," I'm not referring to the Teton Valley's senior citizens. Instead, I'm referring to people in their late 20s and 30s.

These are people who may have purchased property in Victor or Driggs a few years ago, when they were single or newly married. In the past few years, however, quality of life for these folks has become more

Continued on next page

TETON STYLE

Victor rancher cultivates winter-hardy fruits. See page 5B.
Wednesday, July 19, 1995

Team leader Candace Collins tops off a new National Elk Refuge boundary marker with a fresh coat of orange paint. A 10-member team of the National Civilian Community Corps, part of President Clinton's Americorps, is working on the refuge this summer.

VOLUNTEERS OF AMERICORPS

■ Clinton program sees workers doing jobs the government wouldn't otherwise complete.

By Mark Huffman

At the north end of the National Elk Refuge, Lori Hazle and Heidi Rammer had hiked into an area open only to elk, buffalo and other wildlife, up a steep, dusty slope, hauling gallon-sized cans.

They topped the butte, glanced a moment at the Tetons spread across the horizon and turned to the reason they'd come. In a moment they had the cans open, and, brushes in hand, began slopping bright orange paint on four-inch posts that bore Elk Refuge boundary signs.

In the distance, there were more posts, and past those more, and still more beyond, stretching to the edge of view.

"The painting is really a lot easier than lugging the posts up here," Hazle said. "We brought them in and took out the old ones, dug out the holes and put these in."

The old signs "were leaning from having the bison leaning on them," Hazle said.

Hazle, a 21-year-old Denver native with plans to become a veterinary tech, and Rammer, 23, a Wellesley grad with a geology degree, were soon flecked with sweat and paint as they went about their work on one of the posts. More than 60 had been replaced in the previous days, the work done by hand.

"These people really work hard," said team leader Candace Collins, 26 and with three years working for the Peace Corps in West Africa behind her. "This is really labor intensive; my arms are getting really strong."

Across the sage-covered slope where Collins was brushing, members of the group were painting other posts that they had set. It was work the United States Fish and Wildlife Service needed to have done, but that had gone undone because of lack of people and money.

Instead, it was Collins, Hazle, Rammer and eight other members of Americorps that were doing the work. All are members of the National Civilian Community Corps.

Continued on page 8B

VIEW from the HOLE
MARK HUFFMAN

From the silent depths of space, whining noises

Deep in dark space on a mission beyond the mere safety of Earth, three men suddenly find themselves facing a challenge greater than what ordinary men ever think of overcoming.

Far past the reach of any help, they suddenly are imperiled by a crisis that will test their abilities, their skills, their very fiber as men. Their future depends

only and entirely on what they can do to save themselves.

I know. Sounds like that new movie about Apollo 13, the third American flight to the moon, the mission on which an oxygen tank exploded and left our men low on air, power, fuel, everything except resourcefulness and guts.

But it also sounds like something else, though the

news has been kept pretty much hushed. It sounds, if I may dare break the near silence, like the recent mission of Mir, the Russian space station, and its apparently unwelcome guest, American astronaut Norman Thagard.

The fight was designed to link the American and Russian space programs, to put us on their spaceship and them

on ours, to inspire new interest and support for our probing of the bleak cosmos, the great black empty that stretches from our home to forever. It didn't turn out so well.

Instead, Thagard returned to earth and said he had a very unpleasant stay on Mir, and two Russian space guys with whom Thagard spent

Continued on page 18B

Excursion – 4
Popcult – 8
At the Movies – 19
Calendar – 20

Jackson Hole News
July 26 - August 1, 1995

Go exhibit-hopping on Gallery Night this Friday. See page 11.

Stepping Out

ENTERTAINMENT, RECREATION AND THE ARTS

BEST BETS

■ **Widespread Panic.** Fans of southern "space jazz" rock should turn out this weekend to see Widespread Panic at Snow King Center. As Panic matures and tightens up its sound, more people are comparing the group to great southern rockers such as Marshall Tucker and the Allman Brothers, says music writer Porter Fox. See page 3.

■ **Classical kids.** As part of its education and outreach program, the Grand Teton Music Festival is having a Young People's Concert. Ling Tung will conduct excerpts from Tchaikovsky's Polonaise and Waltz from the opera *Eugene Onegin* and Symphony No. 2. See page 7.

■ **Eclectic guitar.** Guitarist Paul Chasman dabbles in many genres when it comes to playing his instrument, from blues to ragtime to bluegrass. Chasman will give a concert sponsored by the Music Conservatory in which he will play Prokofiev's *Seventh Piano Sonata* transcribed for guitar. See page 9.

Paul Chasman

■ **Vocal acrobatics.** The Hennes Gallery and the Jackson Hole Fine Arts Guild are sponsoring a "Musical Afternoon" this weekend. Special guest tenor Tim Wilson from the Metropolitan Opera will join pianist Christine Rogers, baritone Richard Albrecht, soprano Laura Turner and Sarah J. Weber, and mezzo soprano Bev Wanner. See page 15.

More than just
Fair to Midway

Neon lights up the Teton County Fairgrounds. See page 5 for a complete schedule of Fair events.

VIEWPOINTS

EDITORIAL

River deaths raise questions of safety

The loss of two boaters on the Snake and Hoback rivers in the last three weeks raises disturbing questions about safety on the valley's waterways. On May 30, Kyle Martin, an inexperienced kayaker, drowned in the Hoback after venturing downstream alone. Last week, Mary McGavock, a member of a Utah church group, disappeared in the Snake after the raft she was in snagged on a rock and dumped its load.

In the face of these deaths, public agencies must wrestle with the split ethic peculiar to rugged western lands. The spirit of adventure won't survive amidst an over-regulated bureaucracy, yet there is some obligation to counsel the public against seasonal hazards that suddenly arise.

There are several programs in the Yellowstone area that blend education, registration and freedom. In Grand Teton National Park, the trend in mountaineering has been to move away from registration. Now day climbers are asked to leave their itinerary with friends on rugged runs don't have to act as baby sitters. Yet the Jenny Lake ranger station remains a clearinghouse for information on high-altitude conditions and the place to register for multi-day ascents.

In that same park, almost all boaters have a face-to-face contact with a ranger annually when receiving a park boat permit. This allows the dissemination of safety information and regulations. In Yellowstone, people who receive a permit for an overnight excursion may be required to view a short video program. It covers topics about food storage, grizzly bears, swift-moving rivers and creeks, dangerous afternoon winds on high altitude lakes and other perils.

The Bridger-Teton National Forest can look to its own offices to see a highly regarded program that classifies danger in the backcountry on a daily basis. The avalanche hot line is used hundreds of times a day by skiers who venture off the groomed slopes looking for untracked powder. It has undoubtedly saved lives — how many we can only guess.

The popular Snake River Canyon poses a different sort of problem for the Bridger-Teton. Many of those who use it most at risk are out-of-town novices. Yet most pass a single point — the West Table Creek boat launching site — where information about river conditions can be easily disseminated. Young, inexperienced-looking boaters with rented equipment launching during high water are obvious targets for safety lectures.

As the Bridger-Teton contemplates a permit system that would limit use in the canyon, it might consider river danger as another reason for changing the existing free-for-all. Obtaining a permit would guarantee contact with a ranger who could review current conditions. If another regulation is to be imposed, it might as well be used to add to the safety of the public.

LETTERS

Function's the thing

Reference: The parking lot at the new Teton County-Jackson Recreation Center — a capital facilities tax project.

Land for parking: Form should follow function.

The new recreation center with its pools and water slide was designed with its intended use in mind. The layout seems to work very well with all the different activities going on at the same time.

The outside of the Rec Center should be a parking lot, not some architect's summer show piece. We are in the west now — build a parking lot for cars, not trees. We can look up and see the trees on the mountains. We need parking in the summer and should be able to plow it in the winter. Why waste valuable ground?

Let form follow function on the outside as well.

Harry Washut
Moran

Enough, already

Before I went on vacation, there were a few businesses that wanted to receive liquor licenses, a town that wants to give them out on a meritorious scale. Then the budget for the city has to be decided, and lo and behold, the great budgeters want to trim some of the fat by cutting back funding to a few of the substance-abuse businesses that seem to get no respect.

Evidence has proven that alcohol

and drug abuse lead to a number of criminal behavior anomalies that, when left to continue, escalate to unfathomable levels. Don't we have enough bars and drive-through liquor stores here already?

I am not against the consumption of alcohol or the selling of it. But why do we need to unbalance the system that seems to be working?

Benjamin Wilson
Jackson Hole

P.S. I noticed the graduating class pictures in the paper, and the cap with the beer caps was a fitting tribute to what at least one grad is planning to do...

Pork park funding

People from around Yellowstone National Park should be concerned about pork-barrel parks and the impact they have on nationally significant parts of the National Park Service.

Former Park Service Director James Ridenour outlined how members of Congress have developed pork parks around the country in order to please their constituents. The pork parks are not nationally significant but have been created to direct federal funding to particular congressional districts. Unfortunately, they have come at the expense of national parks such as Yellowstone, Yosemite and Independence Hall.

Major Park Service units have not received adequate funds for basic maintenance of their facilities while new parks are created. Now that Congress is finally scrutinizing the federal budget and looking at some of these problems in the Park Service,

Continued on page 22A

Weather Picture

QUOTE OF THE WEEK:
"It's smoke and mirrors, and the voters aren't going to be fooled."

— Bed tax critic Bill Phelps on a plan to increase the tax and use it more liberally.

Write now

Letters to the editor should be signed and include a telephone number for verification. Keep 'em short; we will edit for length. No thank yous, thank you. Guest editorials are limited to 700 words. Write Box 1445, Jackson, Wyo., 83001 or fax to (307) 733-2138 or e-mail to jhnews@wyoming.com.

Publisher
Michael Sellett
Editor
Angus Morrison Thuermer Jr.
Associate Editor
Mark Huffman
Art Director
Eileen Kaplan Benedyk
News and Features
Thomas Dewell
Roger Hayden
Matt Inyak
Alison Gregor
Page Layout and Design
Cameron Fox
Dorothy Verbovszky
Chief Photographer
Garth Dowling
Staff Photographers
Michele Bauer
Darkroom Tech
Fine Wilson
Copy Editor
Sharon Rudd
Advertising Director
Wayne Marvin
Advertising Sales
Mary Lohuis
Vic Gann
Advertising Sales Assistant
Valerie Black
Ad Production Manager
Janet Melvin
Ad Design
Anita Baron
Lyn Coffey
Alison Gillentine
Typesetter
Nancy Perry
Printing Production Manager
John Wright
Press Foreman
John Zumwalt
Pressmen
Greg Gruetzmacher
Press Assistant
Brian Wetz
Process Darkroom
Michelle Bauer
Mailroom
Tammy Thurman
Office Manager
Teresa Thomas
Receptionist
Jenny Wiggan

Le Devoir
Montreal, Canada

El uso de los colores. "Es necesario garantizar que el color se utilice en una forma más natural," dijo Peter Bhatia, gerente administrador de The Oregonian, Portland, Oregon. "Debe ser parte de la identidad básica del periódico, pero no debe utilizarse sólo por el gusto de utilizar el color en una página."

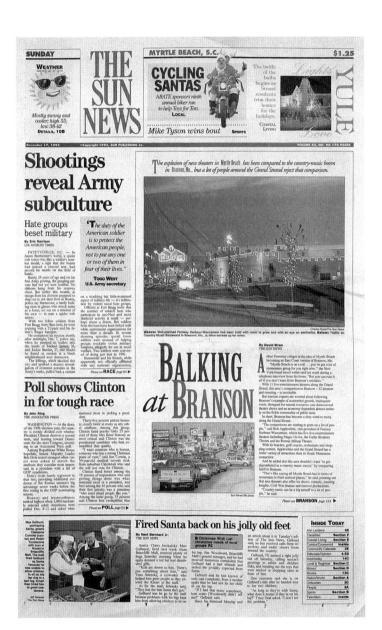

The Sun News
Myrtle Beach, SC

Use of space. "I think we're starting to use our space much better than we ever have," said Marty Petty, senior vice president and general manager, The Hartford (Conn.) Courant. "We're writing and editing more tightly, assigning graphics more judiciously, and, generally, packaging the paper smarter."

'LIFE IN SHOALS' INTRODUCES FOLKS FROM ACROSS REGION. INSIDE 1E-10H

Roy Phillips and his wife, Helen, make extra effort on paper route.

CARVER HOMES BOYS AND GIRLS CLUB DIRECTOR LIFTS PROGRAM. REGION 1B

1D Childbirth courses prepare women for delivery, but there's little support for mothers after the child is born.

NEIGHBOR'S MAID TESTIFIES VIA CAMERA IN SIMPSON TRIAL. NATION 2A

TimesDaily

50¢ Newsstand • Tuesday, February 28, 1995 • Serving Northwest Alabama since 1869

TODAY'S WEATHER
Storms likely with some hump.
High 67. Low tonight 57.
Complete report on page 2A.

Lauderdale raises rate for garbage collection

By Robert Palmer
Staff Writer

$10 A MONTH

BE PREPARED
'Seconds save lives'

Threatening weather a fact of life in Alabama

By Dennis Sherer
Staff Writer

BIRTH OF A TORNADO

Sheriff: Financial disaster prevented

Volunteer work saved department, Plott says

By Tom Smith and Mike Goens
of the TimesDaily

"Fortunately, we've had great support. ... I don't know where we'd be without them."
LARRY PLOTT
Franklin County Sheriff

INSIDE

Florence, Alabama
Volume 126, Number 59
Copyright © 1995 TimesDaily Inc.

Ann Landers 2D
Business 8A
Calendar 2D
Classified 5C
Comics 4D
Crossword 7C
Horoscope 4D

Life 10
Obituaries 2B
Opinion 8B
Region 1B
Sports 1C
Television 2D
Weather 2A

Sometimes, the coaches are as much fun to watch as the game.
PAGE 1C

For home delivery of the TimesDaily call (205) 766-3434

1996 GOP PRESIDENTIAL RACE
Alexander assumes outsider role

By John King
AP Political Writer

NASHVILLE, Tenn.

Marines land on Somalia to aid U.N. peacekeepers

By Reid G. Miller
Associated Press

MOGADISHU, Somalia

C
TUESDAY
FEB. 28, 1995
TimesDaily

Sports

SIGNED
Reds have some fun by signing former star Pedro Borbon from team's glory days.
PAGE 3C

STATE TOURNAMENT
► Shoals Stallions anxious to advance past state level. 3C

NCAA
NCAA 4C
ALSO INSIDE
■ CLASSIFIEDS/SC

JERRY FELTS

Louganis: A coward or a hero?

HIGH SCHOOL BASKETBALL

Players, owners talking

By Ronald Blum
AP Sports Writer

SCOTTSDALE, Ariz.

SIDELINE
Hysteria

Coaches offer own show during games

By Gregg Dewalt
Assistant Sports Editor

HANCEVILLE

Cophia Rutherford removes her blazer after a call went against the Lady Hornets.

Lexington's Ricky Bryan covers his eyes after his team made a mistake against Northside.

Clutch shooting keys Lady Vikings' victory

By Lance Hyche
For the TimesDaily

BOAZ

Lady Stallions escape with last-second win

By Lance Hyche
For the TimesDaily

BOAZ

Walter Raney's Lady Stallions needed a last-second shot to beat Faulkner Monday.

D
TUESDAY
FEB. 28, 1995
TimesDaily

Life

TIMELY TIP

BIRTH of a CRISIS

Childbirth, other pre-natal courses prepare women for delivery, but there's little support for mothers after the child is born

JANE BRODY

About

TimesDaily
Florence, AL

La utilización del espacio. "Creo que estamos comenzando a utilizar nuestro espacio mucho mejor que nunca," dijo Marty Petty, vice presidente principal y gerente general de The Hartford Courant, de Connecticut. "Estamos escribiendo y corrigiendo más estrictamente; distribuyendo mas juiciosamente las gráficas y, en general, disponiendo los periódicos de una manera más inteligente."

Region

TRI-STATE Report

SHEFFIELD

Police seeking robbery suspect

Police were continuing an investigation around midnight Monday into a residential robbery in which a man assaulted two elderly women and took an undetermined amount of cash.

Officers said the man accosted a residence in the 1600 block of Crestline Avenue shortly after 9 p.m. after knocking on the door, telling the women he had car trouble and asking to use their telephone.

Upon entering the house, the man roughed up the women, described the place, took their money and left on foot, heading west toward the Sixth Mart convenience store at the corner of Sixth Boulevard and Crestline.

Both women were taken to a nearby hospital, where they were treated and released from the emergency room, according to police. Officers said they suffered facial lacerations, bumps and bruises, but their injuries were not life-threatening.

Police in Sheffield and Florence were questioning a possible suspect after a similar incident occurred at a Florence residence a short period later. The suspect had earlier been reported to be a white male wearing a baseball cap but no shirt or shorts.

The person suspected of the robbery in Florence also reportedly used a chain saw, police said.

The person suspected of the robbery in Florence also reportedly fled his victim on foot, heading to the woods where they confided to Florence police that they had lost him in custody.

BRISTOL, TENN.

6th-grader files $200,000 lawsuit

A sixth-grade student has filed a $200,000 lawsuit against her sixth-education teacher, the school board and Sullivan County, accusing the teacher of calling her a "naked child."

The lawsuit filed by Krystan Hope Webster, 12, and her mother Barbara White alleges the remark was repeated twice in class in November and once to the girl's mother.

Roy Burroughs, the teacher at Bountville Middle School who allegedly made the remark, declined comment, as did County Attorney Dan Street and Pat Hull, an attorney for the Sullivan County Board of Education.

— *Associated Press*

BCA again seeking to limit liability

Frivolous suits, large verdicts target of reform

By Dana Beyerle
Montgomery Bureau

JAMES continued on 2B

HUNTSVILLE FACILITY

Storm clouds still obscure NWS office

By Dennis Sherer
Staff Writer

NEXRAD coverage of Alabama

MARY BEAN

Mover and shaker

Carver club director making things happen

By Lena Mitchell
Staff Writer

FLORENCE — She has been referred to as Mother Goose, the Woman Who Lived in the Shoe, and the Pied Piper all rolled into one, but in reality she is club director for the Carver Home Boys and Girls Club.

Since Mary Bean assumed the director's post Oct. 1, 1994, membership and participation in programs at the club have increased, invigorating has expanded and community support has climbed, according to Michael Socarras, director of the Boys and Girls Clubs in Northwest Alabama.

"Mary Bean has not been a godsend," Socarras said. "Her job really is the children's needs and giving them the elements they need to be a healthy, productive people are just right on target. What she's doing is at the heart of the Boys and Girls Club philosophy."

Just last week, about 30 children at the club attended a black history program to learn about scientists and inventors from a music classic and a female classical engineer.

By the end of the week, many of these same children dressed in their best to perform songs and readings for their families and friends during a black history program.

Creating a cooperative spirit

"The Boys and Girls Club is a positive place for kids," Bean said. "It's an alternative to the streets, and we hope what we're doing will enrich the school system as well as the children."

Investors said a key asset Bean has brought to her role is the ability to build coalitions.

"One of the best things she's done is the cooperative spirit she's helped to create with the community, letting them know what we're doing, coordinating with schools, counselors, juvenile probation officers, just creating a continuum for those children," she said.

Florence real estate agent Beryl Wilson said it was the enormous energy, love and creativity he sees in Bean that propelled him to help with one of her projects — Project

Women get 2 key posts in Cabinet

The Associated Press

Shoals jobless rate rises from record December low

By Carl Cowan
Assistant Regional Editor

PROGRAM continued on 2B

El País de las Tentaciones received Best of Show and JSR for resisting the temptation of typographic excess. Judges cited the publication for the finest example of artful restraint.

Gold
• For Feature Page
El País de las Tentaciones
Madrid, Spain
Nuria Muiña, Designer; Wladimir Marnich, Designer; Ignacio Rubio, Designer; Miguel Gener, Photo Editor; Vicente Jiménez, Editor; Fernando Gutiérrez, Designer

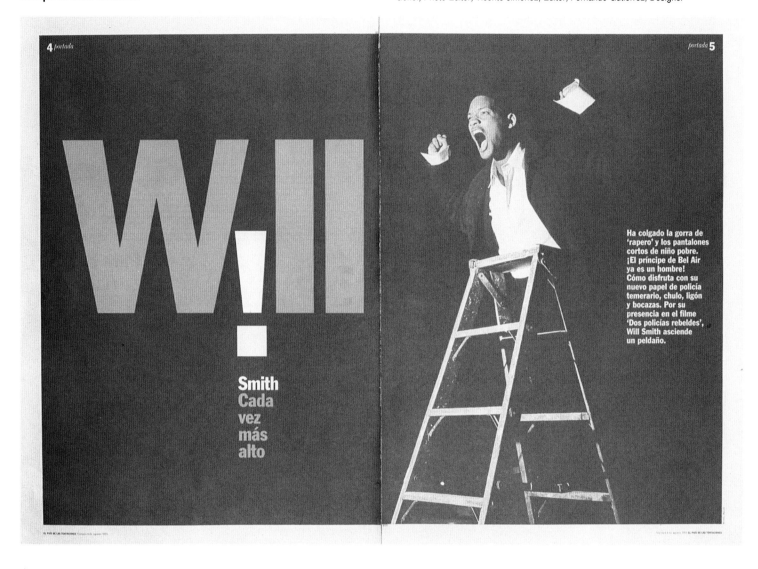

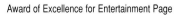

Award of Excellence for Entertainment Page

Award of Excellence for Feature Page

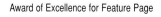

Silver for Feature Page

Silver for Feature Page

6 *rostros*

Ruper Ordorika es un rockero con las ideas claras y los pies en el suelo, su suelo: Euskadi. Esconde su mirada tímida tras unas gafas pasadas de moda. ¿Qué ve?: las 5.700 culturas sepultadas por la historia, el 'crack', los emigrantes árabes... Todo lo canta en un perfecto euskera.

Podría pasar por un científico despistado, un profesor universitario, o por un poeta anclado en sus propias emociones, pero nada estaría más lejos de la verdad: Ruper Ordorika es uno de los rockeros hispanos con las ideas más claras y los pies más anclados en la tierra, su tierra: Euskadi. Si alguien lo dudaba (o todavía desconocía su nombre), *Se' ik so'*, su último disco, es una demostración clara, palpable, y, sobre todo, audible.

Se trata del quinto disco en solitario de este vasco tímido y apacible que se esconde tras unas gafas de montura deliberadamente posada de moda y habla pausadamente como si el mundo, incluido el rock, ya no tuviera prisa. En realidad, Ruper Ordorika nunca ha tenido prisa, no se ha tomado su profesión de cantante y compositor como una carrera de velocidad, sino como una prueba de fondo, y el tiempo le ha dado la razón: no ha conseguido (todavía) ningún número uno, pero a sus 39 años recién cumplidos puede presumir de una de las trayectorias más coherentes y consecuentes de un panorama, el nuestro, que no destaca precisamente por su coherencia.

Hace ya algunos años Ruper Ordorika colgó un letrero en la puerta de su local de ensayo: "Aquí se toca *tuff* and *tuff*". En aquel momento era una declaración de intenciones en un entorno que entendía el rock como algo extraño,

ajeno. Eran momentos en los que el panorama cultural vasco no admitía medias tintas: cantar en euskera era una toma de postura y hacer rock otra, y todavía no estaba claro que pudieran superponerse. "Comencé cantando en inglés e intentando tocar la batería", recuerda Ordorika con una sonrisa contenida que denota más asombro por lo que pasó que añoranza de algún tipo. "La verdad es que necesité bastantes años para llegar a pensar que podía hacer algo que me gustaba en mi idioma. Esa es una de las muchas cosas que les debo a los que, en ese momento, ya cantaban en euskera y habían sido capaces de crear algo que para mí era vanguardista: cantar en euskera y asociarlo con la canción tradicional, que para mí ahora parece más o menos normal, pero que entonces, para mí, fue una revelación. En el País Vasco tenemos la suerte de tener unos patriarcas que han trabajado con mucho rigor y que no han pasado una pelota muy bien elaborada. Cuando yo asomé la cabeza a la música, me encontré con una canción en euskera que me emocionó mucho eso, sumado al hilo de mi tiempo, el rock, es lo que ha conformado mi personalidad musical".

Primeros pasos

A los 21 años Ordorika dio sus primeros pasos musicales serios colaborando con el entonces aún desconocido Bernardo Atxaga. Profundidad de textos y rock se entremezclaban en lo que Ordorika recuerda como "una decisión muy extravagante". "Era una época en la que lo peor era ser cantante y encima en euskera. Como todavía el punk no nos había llegado, nos apuntamos al rock. No recuerdo ya los móviles extramusicales que nos empujaron, pero lo hube cantar en euskera está muy cerca del compromiso (ya sé que es una palabra que está completamente en desuso, pero es así), se requiere un posicionamiento previo, la gente que lo oye capta que es una actitud muy premeditada y, si no se entiende, piensa que es algo político".

Las canciones de Ruper Ordorika están fuertemente ancladas en su realidad cotidiana, en el tiempo que le ha tocado vivir, pero nada tienen de panfleto social (y mucho menos político): el rock vendido en las esquinas ("el malestar / vuela como el aburrido pájaro de la tarde: todo es ahora sueño, olvido, / muerte dulce"), las 5.700 culturas que ya han desaparecido a lo largo de la historia ("no, no hay que olvidar / que todas esas culturas / sólo eran una traba / para el progreso. No, no hay que olvidarlo, / esas cinco mil y pico / culturas desaparecidas / no podían estar equivocadas"), los emigrantes árabes que atraviesan España para pasar sus vacaciones en familia ("ellos marchan, es un viaje. / Yo también marcho, también estoy de viaje, / pero no sé si encontraré mi verdadera casa, no sé si la encontraré") o simplemente el discurrir de cada día ("Acaso, quizás, seguramente, / no sé, puede ser, de alguna manera, / Éste es el léxico que más se usa / ya no hay decisiones, / y la gente se queda en casa"). ■ Miguel Jurado

Se' Ik so' acaba de ser editado por Nuevos Medios.

EL PAIS
NÚMERO 106

K.D. LANG
SE GUSTA

DE LAS
TENTACIONES

CINE: Easy Rawlins, un detective de color para el mejor cine negro. Entrevista a **William Hurt:** "En EE UU te pagan por hacer mierda".
MÚSICA: Black Grape molesta al Papa. ¡Resucitado!: **Mercury, Cobain** y **Lennon** vuelven de la tumba. **TEATRO:** 24 horas en la vida de 'Krámpack'. **VIAJES:** Azores.

EL PAIS
NÚMERO 114
Viernes 29 de diciembre 1995

LA MEJOR
Los lectores eligen a Rosario artista musical del 95

DE LAS
TENTACIONES

CÓMIC: el bueno de Cuttlas te regala su calendario para 1996. **NOCHEVIEJA:** las mejores ofertas para despedir el año.
VIAJES: Venecia, el invierno más hermoso en la ciudad más implacable. **AGENDA PERSONAL:** las novedades en libros, vídeos y videojuegos.

Silver for Feature Page

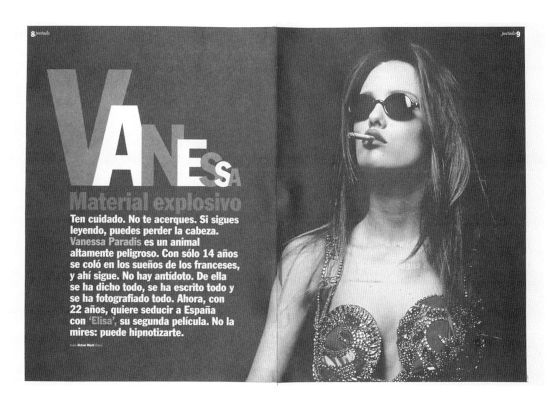

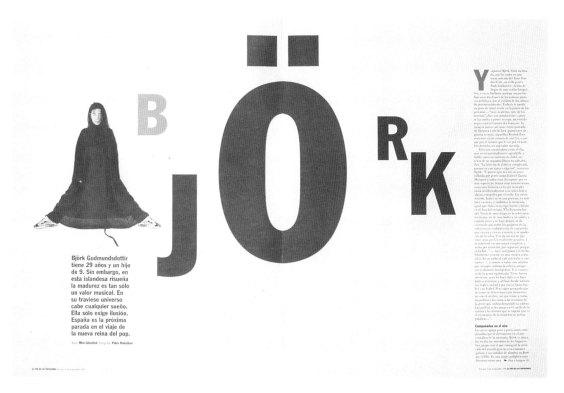

Silver for Feature Page

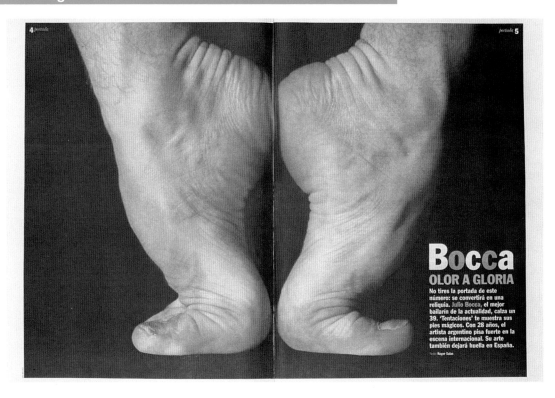

Award of Excellence for Entertainment Page

Silver for Feature Page

Silver for Feature Page

Caníbal, psicótico, ladrón, traidor... Viggo escapa del patrón de galán de Hollywood. Su gran amor es la poesía. Y su máximo deseo: rodar de nuevo en español.

Mortensen

vi g g o s

Award of Excellence for Entertainment Page

Pasen y vean. 33 años después, siguen dando caña. Son incombustibles. Con ustedes, sus satánicas majestades, los Rolling

Stones

D

Silver for Feature Page

Michael
lava más blanco

Michael Jackson tiene mil caras: niño y adulto, terrestre y galáctico, bueno y malo, negro y blanco... Repudiado como persona por sus escándalos sexuales, pero reconocido como un genio musical, el cantante intenta limpiar su trono con 'HIStory', un disco reivindicativo que llega en forma de alud.

ESCUCHA SU TALENTO

Award of Excellence for Feature Page

Award of Excellence for Feature Page

Award of Excellence for Feature Page

Award of Excellence for Feature Page

Award of Excellence for Feature Page

Award of Excellence for Feature Page

JSR
The Ball State Daily News
Muncie, IN

The Ball State Daily News won JSR for overall design. The publication "demontrates what can be done in a journalism school with a faculty that is willing to make the commitment to teaching students the effective use of graphics."

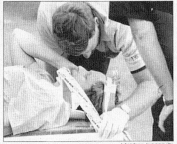

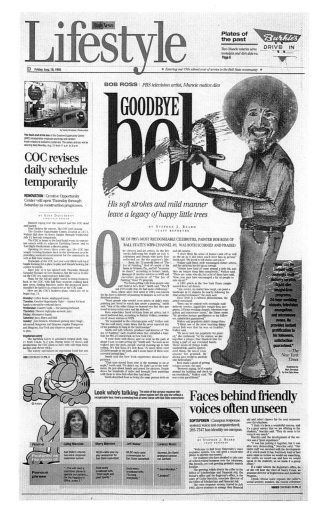

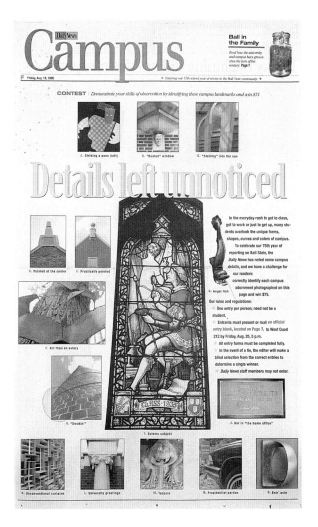

The Palm Beach Post won JSR for content and design of Native Florida. Judges cited vision, technical expertise, outstanding presentation and breadth of work.

Award of Excellence & JSR
The Palm Beach Post
West Palm Beach, FL
John Lopinot, Photographer; Mark Buzek, Designer; Mark Edelson, Photo Editor; Pat Morgan, Accent Editor; Melissa Segrest, AME Features; Steve Madden, Artist

The Detroit News — MetroLife newspaper section and Horror in Oklahoma section

Award of Excellence
The Detroit News
Detroit, MI
Dale Peskin, DME; Chris Kozlowski, Design Editor; Chris Willis, Assistant Graphics Editor; Shayne Bowman, Assistant Design Editor; David Kordalski, Assistant Graphics Editor; Joe Gray, Assistant News Editor; Theresa Badovich, Page Designer; Sean McDade, Graphic Artist; Tim Summers, Graphic Artist

The Detroit News won JSR for its daily efforts of storytelling through the use of organization, clear labeling and accessibility of information.

The Detroit News
MetroLife
YOUR GUIDE TO NAVIGATING LIFE IN THE '90S

PAGE 1D   FRIDAY, JUNE 9, 1995

PEST CONTROL
Mosquitoes: The worst is yet to come

Cutting red tape

COMING MONDAY
Chick chic?

Vintner offers advice on wedding toasts with spirit

HELMET SAFETY

Jonathan Hughes wears a Bell Razor Pump helmet and holds the Bell Reflector, which offers greater protection along the neck.

Use your head when it comes to bicycle safety

What's hot and what's not

Best 'Razor & Avalanche' Pump

Better Troxel 'Diva'

Good: Trek 'AstralZX'

O.J. VERDICT ★ EVIDENCE
Wednesday, October 4, 1995 | The Detroit News | 12A

Keys to the crime: Blood, gloves, socks, hair

Jurors in the O.J. Simpson murder trial had access to 50,000 pages of evidence and more than 1,000 exhibits.

The crime scene: Nicole Brown Simpson's condo

The search: O.J.'s Brentwood mansion

Blood in the Bronco

THURSDAY, APRIL 20, 1995   THE DETROIT NEWS   3A

Horror in Oklahoma

Downtown Detroit
Fear grips McNamara building

Hundreds of workers flee after phoned bomb threat to IRS offices

By Francis Hopkins and Allan Lengel
The Detroit News

Nicole McClain, a legal clerk in the Social Security office, waits for a ride after the building was evacuated.

Some workers inside the McNamara rush out of the building after the telephoned bomb threat Wednesday.

Robert Sumner of the Detroit Police K-9 unit and his dog prepare to enter the McNamara to check the threat. The K-9 unit found no bomb.

The Associated Press contributed to this report.

Security
Experts offer tips to fight terrorist acts

Vigilance, training have to be part of a response to bomb threats.

By John Bebow
The Detroit News

Reaction
Day-care workers frightened: 'It could happen anywhere'

By Said Deep
The Detroit News

How to help

SEVENTEENTH EDITION   61

Silver & JSR
Le Soleil
Québec, Canada
Lucie Lacava, Design Consultant; Jean-Pascal Beaupré, Front Page; Staff, Inside pages; Gilbert Lacasse, President and Editor; Majella Soucy, AME; Michel Samson, AME; Desk Staff, Inside pages

Le Soleil won JSR for overall redesign and the originality in the way the redesign embraces content.

After

Before

After

After

After

QUESTIONS D'ARGENT

LE SOLEIL — LE MERCREDI 1ER NOVEMBRE 1995 — CAHIER C

Le huard s'envole

Les taux hypothécaires baisseront

Le CRTC approuve l'augmentation de 2$ pour les appels locaux

Le Permanent: un règlement à l'amiable demeure possible

FINANCES PERSONNELLES ET FAMILIALES

Attention à l'euphorie

OPINIONS

LE QUOTIDIEN DE LA CAPITALE

Pas de décision précipitée, M. Bouchard

Démagogie et appel au racisme

CARREFOUR DES LECTEURS

J'ai été choquée

On me vole un cadeau

Jacques Parizeau, gaffeur, fier et rationnel

ARTS ET SPECTACLES ○ VOTRE AGENDA

CAHIER B — LE SOLEIL — LE MERCREDI 1ER NOVEMBRE 1995

MAGAZINE

PARIZEAU DÉMISSIONNE

20 minutes comme chauffeur de Parizeau

Jacques Parizeau avait cette allure de fier hidalgo quand il a adhéré au PQ, en septembre 1969.

LISE LACHANCE
Le Soleil

UN LONG PARCOURS

GILBERT LEDUC
Le Soleil

Cette photo fut prise en 1977. À cette période, Jacques Parizeau était ministre des Finances. Il avait occupé le poste prestigieux de conseiller économique et financier du gouvernement du Québec sous plusieurs premiers ministres, dont le libéral Jean Lesage.

En 1982, Jacques Parizeau était ministre des Finances. Sur cette photo, il discute, avec le premier ministre du Parti québécois de l'époque René Lévesque, du projet de loi sur l'augmentation des salaires des membres de l'Assemblée nationale.

CURRICULUM VITAE

Voir PARCOURS en B3 ►

Voir CHAUFFEUR en B3 ►

Silver & JSR
Asbury Park Press
Neptune, NJ
Russ DeSantis, Photographer; Harris
Siegel, ME Design & Photography,
Designer; Andrew Prendimano, Art &
Photo Director; Don Wilno, Copy
Editor; John Quinn, ME Sports

Asbury Park Press won JSR for innovation in sports
design.

In this chapter judges recognize outstanding design for front pages, local news pages, sports pages, business pages, inside pages and other news pages. Breaking news pages include local/regional, national and international. Special news topics must represent one theme and are divided into local/regional, national and international.

News

- **News Sections**
- **News Pages**
- **Breaking News Pages**
- **Special News Topics**

Silver
O'Globo
Rio De Janeiro, Brazil
Mario Marona, Deputy Managing Editor; Claudio Prudente, Design Editor & Designer

Award of Excellence
The Atlanta Journal and Constitution
Atlanta, GA
Tony DeFeria, Designer & AME Graphics/Photography;
Marlene Karas, Photographer

PAZ

A cidade se une hoje contra a violência, na caminhada
Reage Rio, a partir das 16h, da Candelária à Cinelândia

Seqüestradores assassinaram executivo

Award of Excellence
Chicago Tribune
Chicago, IL
Staff

Award of Excellence
Detroit Free Press
Detroit, MI
Wayne Kamidoi, Design Director & Designer

Award of Excellence
The Detroit News
Detroit, MI
Dale Peskin, Deputy Managing Editor; Joe Gray, Assistant
News Editor; Theresa Badovich, Page Designer

Award of Excellence
The Detroit News
Detroit, MI
Shayne Bowman, Asst. Design/Graphics Editor; Michael
Kellams, Sports Designer; Alan Whitt, Deputy Sports
Editor; Chris Kozlowski, Design/Graphics Director

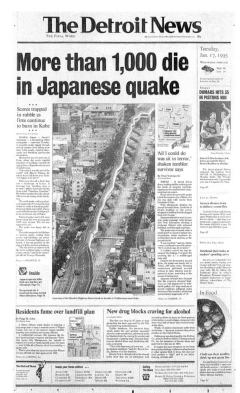

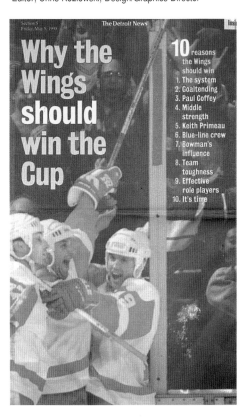

Award of Excellence
Diario de Noticias
Huarte-Pamplona, Spain
Javier Errea, Art Director & Designer; Francisco J. Zudaire,
ME

Award of Excellence
Diario de Noticias
Huarte-Pamplona, Spain
Javier Errea, Art Director & Designer; Francisco J.
Zudaire, ME

Award of Excellence
• Also Award of Excellence for Breaking News
The Detroit News
Detroit, MI
Dale Peskin, DME; Chris Kozlowski, Design Editor; Chris
Willis, David Kordalski, Asst. Graphics Editors; Shayne
Bowman, Asst. Design Editor; Joe Gray, Asst. News Editor;
Theresa Badovich, Page Designer; Sean McDade, Tim
Summers, Graphic Artist

Award of Excellence
The Home News
East Brunswick, NJ

Christine Birch, Designer; Harris Siegel, ME/Design & Photography, Designer; Tom Kerr, Art Director; Teresa Klink, ME/News; Michael Goldfinger, Photographer; Dick Hughes, Editor

Award of Excellence
Jacksonville Journal-Courier
Jacksonville, IL

Mike Miner, Editor/Designer

Award of Excellence
Le Soleil
Québec, Canada

Jean-Pascal Beaupré, AME

Award of Excellence
The Philadelphia Daily News
Philadelphia, PA

John Sherlock, Graphics Editor

Award of Excellence
Ocala Star-Banner
Ocala, FL

Steve Antley, Graphics Editor

Award of Excellence
• Also Award of Excellence for Photojournalism

The Press Democrat
Santa Rosa, CA

Jim Fremgen, Executive News Editor; John Metzger, Photo Director; Chad Surmick, Photographer; Ron Macabe, Layout Editor

Reforma
México City, Mexico
José Luis Barros, Illustrator; José Manuel Mendoza,
Section Designer; Luis Jorge Gallegos, Photographer;
Héctor Moreno, Editor; Ernesto Carrillo, Graphics Editor;
Emilio Deheza, Art Director; Eduardo Danilo, Design
Consultant

Reforma
México City, Mexico
José Manuel Mendoza, Section Designer; Gilberto Avila,
Designer; Raquel Aparicio, Editor; Emilio Deheza, Art
Director; Ernesto Carrillo, Graphics Editor; Eduardo
Danilo, Design Consultant

Reforma
México City, Mexico
José Manuel Mendoza, Section Designer; Miguel Velasco,
Photography; Homero Fernández, Editor; Emilio Deheza,
Art Director; Arturo Jiménez, Graphics Editor; Eduardo
Danilo, Design Consultant

The Seattle Times
Seattle, WA
Bo Hok Cline, News Graphic Designer & Illustrator; David
Miller, Art Director; Christine E. Cox, Art Director &
Illustrator

San Francisco Examiner
San Francisco, CA
Kelly Frankeny, AME Design; Katy Raddatz, Photographer;
George Cant, Sunday Editor; Photo Staff, Art Staff, Staff

San Jose Mercury News
San Jose, CA
Bryan Monroe, AME Graphics/Photography; Jeff Thomas,
Executive News Editor; Scott Demuesy, Photo Editor

Award of Excellence
The Stuart News
Stuart, FL
James Sergent, Chief Designer

Award of Excellence
The Stuart News/Port St. Lucie News
Stuart, FL
Hank Wilson, Deputy Managing Editor; Sanford Myers,
Photographer

Award of Excellence
The Times-Picayune
New Orleans, LA
George Berke, Photographer

Award of Excellence
University Daily Kansan
Lawrence, KS
Noah Musser, Designer; Joann Birk, Reporter; Kathy
Driscoll, Photographer; Colleen McCain, Editor

Award of Excellence
Berlingske Tidende
Copenhagen, Denmark
Carsten Gregersen, Design Editor

ABERDEEN SUNDAY American News

November 19, 1995

House nervous over shutdown

ABERDEEN American News

SATURDAY, April 15, 1995

GIRLS CHANGE CATHOLIC CUSTOM IN SOUTH DAKOTA

Quick fixes unlikely

Clintons expect a handsome tax refund

Fair ticket ruckus may hurt numbers

Burl Ives dies at 85

Award of Excellence
The Oregonian
Portland, OR
Staff

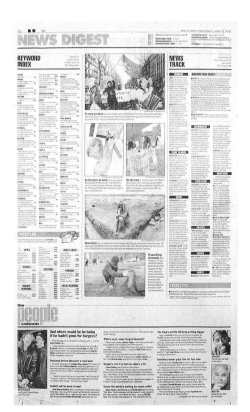

Award of Excellence
The Orange County Register
Santa Ana, CA
Nanette Bisher, AME/Art Director; Maurine Pool, Copy
Editor; Gary Schnurr, Copy Editor; Bill Cunningham, Wire
Editor; John Fabris, Design Team Leader; David Farnham,
Copy Editor

Award of Excellence
• Also Award of Excellence for Breaking News & Special News Topic
The Detroit News
Detroit, MI
Dale Peskin, Deputy ME; Chris Kozlowski, Design &
Graphics Ed.; Chris Willis, Asst. Graphics Ed.; Shayne
Bowman, Asst. Design Ed.; David Kordalski, Asst. Graphics
Ed.; Joe Gray, Asst. News Ed.; Theresa Badovich,
Designer; Daryl Swint, Rob Richards, Graphics Artists;
Brad Sturtz, Auto Ed.; Christopher Bing, Illustrator; Bill
McMillan, News Ed.; Christy Bradford, ME

Award of Excellence
The Sun
Bremerton, WA
Suzette Moyer, Presentation Editor

Award of Excellence
The Detroit News
Detroit, MI
Theresa Badovich, Designer

Award of Excellence
The Virginian-Pilot
Norfolk, VA
Staff

Award of Excellence
The San Diego Union-Tribune
San Diego, CA
Staff

Silver

The New York Times

New York, NY

Corinne Myller, Designer; David Corio, Photographer; Tiina Loite, Photo Editor

Silver

Reforma

México City, Mexico

Daniel Esqueda Guadalajara, Section Designer; Monica Solórzano, Artist; Staff , Photographers; Gustavo Hernández, Editor; Eduardo Danilo, Design Consultant; Arturo Jiménez, Graphics Editor; Emilio Deheza, Art Director

Silver

Duluth News-Tribune

Duluth, MN

Deborah Withey, Art Director; Pat Mcilheran, Copy Editor

Award of Excellence
The New York Times
New York, NY
Joe Zeff, Designer

Award of Excellence
El Norte
Monterrey, Mexico
Adrián Alvarez, Designer; Eddie Macías, Illustrator; Jorge Vidrio, Graphics Editor; Raúl Braulio, Art Director

Award of Excellence
El Norte
Monterrey, Mexico
Adrián Alvarez, Designer; Eddie Macías, Illustrator; Jorge Vidrio, Graphics Editor; Raúl Braulio Martinez, Art Director; Ivonne Orrantia, Claudia Susana Flores, Luis Carlos Martínez, Fernando Luna, Photographers

Award of Excellence
Reforma
México City, Mexico
Daniel Esqueda Guadalajara, Designer; Juan Jesus Cortés, Illustrator; Adrian Rueda, Editor; Ernesto Carrillo, Graphics Editor; Emilio Deheza, Art Director; Eduardo Danilo, Design Consultant

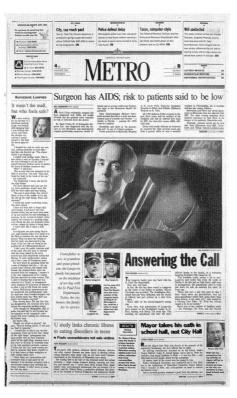

Award of Excellence
Saint Paul Pioneer Press
St. Paul, MN
Ingrid Muller, Designer; Bob McIntosh, News Editor; Lauri Treston, Deputy Visuals Editor/Design; Joe Rossi, Photographer; Bill Alkofer, Photographer

Award of Excellence
The Phoenix Gazette
Phoenix, AZ
Charlie Leight, Design Editor; Peter Schwepker, Photographer; Tim Koors, Photo Editor

The Detroit News ...

The Metro

SECTION D

Your local news section for Friday, June 9, 1995

MetroNews: Gambling backers take their case to Engler. 3D
MetroLife: If mosquitos bug you, try these remedies. 12D

In MetroLife

Grand jury calls Nichols' farmhand

He worked on Decker farm and was drinking buddy of prime suspect McVeigh

Local news at a glance

LANSING
Lawmakers fight over money for Detroit arts

FAITH & PHILOSOPHY

A laughing Jesus? Picture dismays some

SPECIAL REPORT

Perch prices are the limit as fish stock plummets

Special students listen to Grant Hill

FARMINGTON HILLS
Girl at center of nude photo case goes home

More inside
Obituaries ...... Page 2D
Briefs .... Page 3D

Pete Waldmeir ... Page 2D

Contact The News

Fishing ban leaves state's southwest shore high, dry

Silver
The Detroit News
Detroit, MI

Theresa Badovich, Page Designer; Bob Howard, Assistant News Editor; Diana Thomas, Page Designer; Judy Diebolt, City Editor; Shanna Flowers, Assistant City Editor; George Bullard, AME Metro; Rob Richards, Artist

The Detroit News ...

The Metro

SECTION D

In MetroLife
BALLOON FEST

Your local news section for Tuesday, June 20, 1995

MetroNews: Casino developers showcase Hudson's. 3D
MetroLife: Soaring phone service rates anger users. 10D

2 may split reward in rape case

Ann Arbor cabdriver, woman who noticed gloves are top contenders for $100,000

By Robert Ankeny
The Detroit News

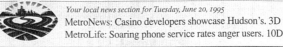

HOWELL
The sky will be heavy with hot air balloons

Local news at a glance

ANN ARBOR
U-M band chief hears new tune in Columbus

ST. CLAIR SHORES

Homeowner feuds with too-close clinic

EAST LANSING
Racetracks betting the farm on slot machines

More inside
Obituaries ...... Page 2D
Briefs .... Page 5D
George Weeks ... Page 4D

Betty DeRamus ... Page 3D

Contact The News

Judy Diebolt
City Editor
222-2100

SPECIAL REPORT

The walking wounded

Children who survive gunshot wounds often face months of rehabilitation to recover from physical and mental injuries.

By James Tobin
The Detroit News

Micah Vincent, 11

Jamie Walker, 14

Jamie Walker, now 14, shoots baskets in her back yard as part of her rehabilitation. Jamie was shot in the head and BB pellets are still lodged in her brain. She is making progress, her mother says.

Where kids were shot

Kids and guns

The Detroit News

MetroLife

YOUR GUIDE TO NAVIGATING LIFE IN THE '90s

COLLECTING ON CALLS

AIR CONDITIONERS

High temps trigger annual stampede

'This is the biggest rush we've had,' retailer says

How to buy an air conditioner

Some pay phone companies under fire for high rates

By Nicole Zdeb
The Detroit News

BALLOON FEST

TECHNOLOGY

Chrysler's home page offers ride down info highway

By Barbara McClellan
The Detroit News

Weekend wandering

FISHING

New lures make it easy to play the baiting game

By James A. McCune
The Detroit News

The sky will be heavy with hot air in Howell

By Barbara McClellan
The Detroit News

SEVENTEENTH EDITION 79

Award of Excellence
The Orange County Register
Santa Ana, CA

Bernadette Finley, Senior Designer; Gary Schnurr, Copy Editor; Maurine Pool, Copy Editor; Nanette Bisher, AME/Art Director

Award of Excellence
San Francisco Examiner
San Francisco, CA

Kelly Frankeny, AME Design; George Cant, Sunday Editor; Marjorie Rice, Graphics Editor; Richard Paoli, Photo Director; Tim Porter, AME News; Photo Staff, Art Staff, News Staff

Award of Excellence
The Virginian-Pilot
Norfolk, VA
Staff

Award of Excellence
The Washington Times
Washington, DC
Joseph W. Scopin, AME Graphics; Paul Watts, Designer; Jennifer Pritchard,
Art Director; Charmaine Roberts, Designer; Glen Stubbe, Photo Director

Silver
• Also Awards of Excellence for Special News Topics & News Portfolio
The Seattle Times
Seattle, WA
David Miller, Art Director; Rick Lund, Design, Editing; Mike Kellams, Graphics, Design; Fred Nelson, Photo
Editor; Cole Porter, Photo Editor; Chris Soprych, Graphics; Cathy Henkel, Editing; Paul Palazzo, Editing;
Photo Staff

THE OTHER VICTIM

Friends praise painter killed in Potomac massacre / 5

TOP OF THE NEWS
Barry says police, schools
can expect to lose jobs / 3

DISTRICT
Board members won't drop
school privatization / 6

MARYLAND
Push for balance on bench
brings backup in courts / 4

VIRGINIA
Gannett foes in McLean
get their day in court / 7

LIFE TIMES
Preserving
America's
legacy / 8

SILVER SPRING DREAM

County eyes megamall / 4

Montgomery County officials and business leaders examine a model of downtown Silver Spring as it might look if a developer gets the go-ahead.

TOP OF THE NEWS
IBM, Toshiba to announce
billion-dollar Va. plant / 3

DISTRICT
Appeals court upholds
Whittington's victory / 6

VIRGINIA
Nissan Pavilion parking,
traffic is a nightmare / 6

LIFE TIMES
Toddler videos fall short
of mesmerizing viewers / 8

MARINER EXTRA

DIVISION PLAYOFFS

GAME 1
AL Championship Series
Mariners vs. Cleveland Indians
Tomorrow: At Kingdome, 5:07 p.m.
TV: KOMO (Channel 4)
Radio: KIRO (710 AM)

MARINERS BEAT YANKEES

Up next: Cleveland
Baseball's best team in
'95 combines speed,
power and pitching.
PAGE E 6

THE SEATTLE TIMES   **SECTION E**   MONDAY, OCTOBER 9, 1995

The Mariner dugout erupts as Ken Griffey Jr. crosses the plate with the winning run in last night's divisional series-clinching game against the Yankees.

Miracle Mariners

*Pair of aces, Edgar's clutch hit
end series for the ages in 11th*

*Seattle holds nothing back
as storybook run continues*

STEVE KELLEY
Times staff columnist

Edgar Martinez is doused with champagne after last night's game.

AL Championship Series
SEATTLE vs. CLEVELAND
Best-of-seven series

Silver
University Daily Kansan
Lawrence, KS
Brian James, Designer

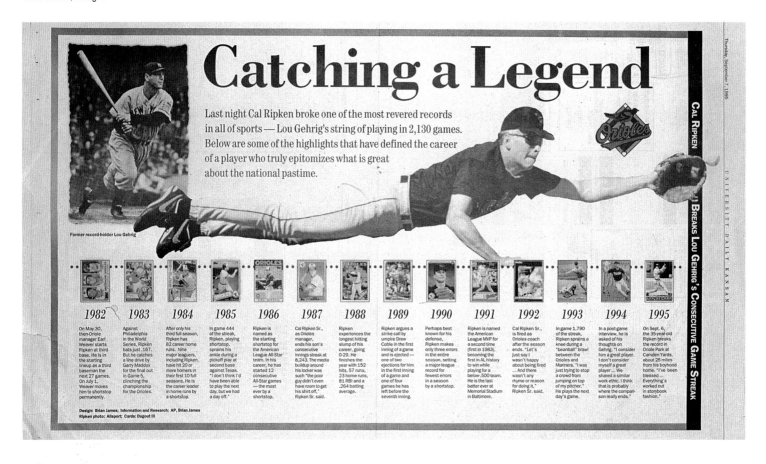

Catching a Legend

Last night Cal Ripken broke one of the most revered records in all of sports — Lou Gehrig's string of playing in 2,130 games. Below are some of the highlights that have defined the career of a player who truly epitomizes what is great about the national pastime.

Former record-holder Lou Gehrig

CAL RIPKEN ► BREAKS LOU GEHRIG'S CONSECUTIVE GAME STREAK

UNIVERSITY DAILY KANSAN

Thursday, September 7, 1995

1982
On May 30, then-Orioles manager Earl Weaver starts Ripken at third base. He is in the starting lineup as a third baseman the next 27 games. On July 1, Weaver moves him to shortstop permanently.

1983
Against Philadelphia in the World Series, Ripken bats just .167. But he catches a line drive by Garry Maddox for the final out in Game 5, clinching the championship for the Orioles.

1984
After only his third full season, Ripken has 82 career home runs. Nine major leaguers, including Ripken, have hit 20 or more homers in their first 10 full seasons. He is the career leader in home runs by a shortstop.

1985
In game 444 of the streak, Ripken, playing shortstop, sprains his ankle during a pickoff play at second base against Texas. "I don't think I'd have been able to play the next day, but we had a day off."

1986
Ripken is named as the starting shortstop for the American League All-Star team. In his career, he has started 12 consecutive All-Star games — the most ever by a shortstop.

1987
Cal Ripken Sr., as Orioles manager, ends his son's consecutive innings streak at 8,243. The media buildup around his locker was such "the poor guy didn't even have room to get his shirt off," Ripken Sr. said.

1988
Ripken experiences the longest hitting slump of his career, going 0-29. He finishes the year with 152 hits, 57 runs, 23 home runs, 81 RBI and a .264 batting average.

1989
Ripken argues a strike call by umpire Drew Coble in the first inning of a game and is ejected — one of two ejections for him in the first inning of a game and one of four games he has left before the seventh inning.

1990
Perhaps best known for his defense, Ripken makes only three errors in the entire season, setting a major-league record for fewest errors in a season by a shortstop.

1991
Ripken is named the American League MVP for a second time (first in 1983), becoming the first in AL history to win while playing for a below-.500 team. He is the last batter ever at Memorial Stadium in Baltimore.

1992
Cal Ripken Sr. is fired as Orioles coach after the season ends. "Let's just say I wasn't happy about being fired ... And there wasn't any rhyme or reason for doing it," Ripken Sr. said.

1993
In game 1,790 of the streak, Ripken sprains a knee during a "beanball" brawl between the Orioles and Mariners. "I was just trying to stop a crowd from jumping on top of my pitcher." He plays the next day's game.

1994
In a post-game interview, he is asked of his thoughts on Gehrig. "I consider him a great player. I don't consider myself a great player ... We shared a similar work ethic. I think that is probably where the comparison really ends."

1995
On Sept. 6, the 35-year-old Ripken breaks the record in Orioles Park at Camden Yards, about 25 miles from his boyhood home. "I've been blessed ... Everything's worked out in storybook fashion."

Design: Brian James; Information and Research: AP, Brian James
Ripken photo: Allsport; Cards: Dugout III

Award of Excellence
AM De Leon
Leon, Mexico
Beatriz Zambrano, Art Director; Gustavo Belman, Designer/Illustrator

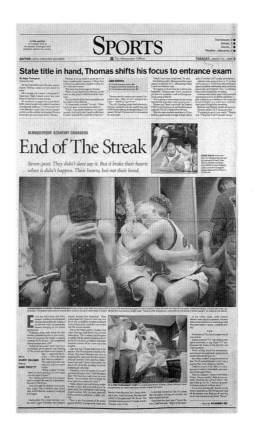

Award of Excellence
The Albuquerque Tribune
Albuquerque, NM
David Carillo, Designer; Marc Piscotty, Photographer

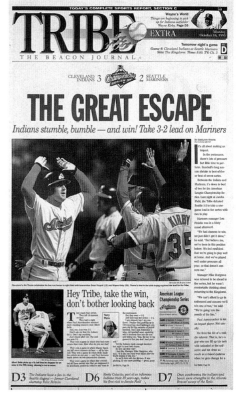

Award of Excellence
Akron Beacon Journal
Akron, OH
Susan Mango Curtis, AME Graphics; Monty Cook, Page Designer; Phil White, Graphic Artist; Bill Eichenberger, Sports Editor

Award of Excellence

Asbury Park Press

Neptune, NJ

Harris Siegel, ME/Design & Photography; Andrew Prendimano, Art & Photo Director; Janet L. Michaud, Designer; Mike Donofrio, Editor; Kevin Shea, Photo Editor; Daryl Stone, Photographer

Award of Excellence

Asbury Park Press

Neptune, NJ

Janet L. Michaud, Designer; Harris Siegel, ME Design & Photography; Andrew Prendimano, Art & Photo Director; Mike Donofrio, Editor

Award of Excellence

Asbury Park Press

Neptune, NJ

Harris Siegel, ME/Design & Photography; Andrew Prendimano, Art & Photo Director; Janet L. Michaud, Designer; Michael Goldfinger, Photographer; John Quinn, ME/Sports

Award of Excellence

Chicago Tribune

Chicago, IL

Stacy Sweat, Graphics Editor; Steve Layton, Artist; Stephen Ravenscraft, Artist; Steve Duenes, Artist

Award of Excellence

Centre Daily Times

State College, PA

Tom Fedor, Photographer; Deborah Withey, Art Director; Dwight Kier, Layout

Award of Excellence

Centre Daily Times

State College, PA

Pat Little, Photographer; Judy Fedor, Photographer; Deborah Withey, Art Director; Jon Tully, Layout

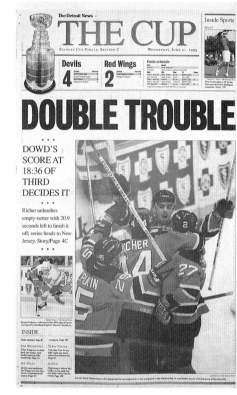

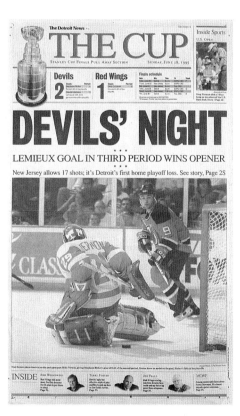

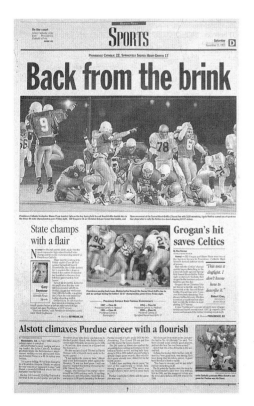

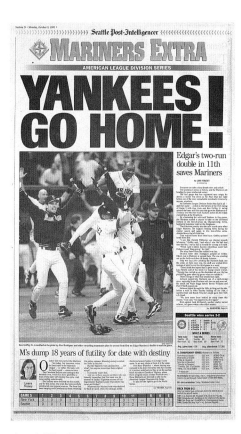

Silver
• Also Award of Excellence for Special Section & News Portfolio & Photo Illustration
The Detroit News
Detroit, MI
Dale Peskin, DME; Chris Kozlowski, Design Editor; Chris Willis, Assistant Graphics Editor; Shayne Bowman, Assistant Design Editor; David Kordalski, Assistant Graphics Editor; Michael Kellams, Sports Designer; Phil Laciura, Sports Editor; Alan Whitt, Deputy Sports Editor; Jerry Harris, Sports Designer; Karen Van Antwerp, Researcher; Jamee Tanner, Graphic Journalist

Left newspaper page (Section D, Sunday, April 9, 1995):

SPORTS

Boxing
McCall outpoints Holmes; Santana leaves on stretcher, but retains his WBC title
D 3

On the move
Hershiser, Abbott, Walker among those shifting teams as baseball frenzy continues
D 8

Husky football
UW's smallest starter steps into some big shoes at spring scrimmage
D 7

Kemp an eyesore for Mavs

Cut-above Sonic ignites big blowout in Big D

Milloy deserves this break

BLAINE NEWNHAM
Times staff columnist

Brian Henninger's birdie on the 16th hole put him 10-under-par for the tournament.

It's high noon for crowded Masters field

'Free-for-all' likely in today's shootout

THE MASTERS

Third-round scores

The leaders

The followers

Others

Television

Inside

O'Brien makes a pit stop at UW

STEVE KELLEY
Times staff columnist

Competing at Husky Stadium is part of Dan O'Brien's spring training. He was seventh in the high jump.

Lower left newspaper page (Seahawks 27, Broncos 10, Monday, October 2, 1995):

SEAHAWKS NOTEBOOK

Struggles continue for Elway

First Bronco TD in eight quarters too little, too late

Seattle cornerback Corey Harris and defensive end Michael Sinclair exult after a turnover thwarted a first-quarter Bronco drive.

Stiff test awaits inspired Seahawks

John Elway is pressured by the Seattle defense while looking to pass in the first-quarter. Elway was smothered and only one touchdown, midway through the final quarter.

Galloway offers big-play potential

Joey Galloway follows the lead of quarterback Rick Mirer. The wide receiver was three receptions and caught four passes, including a 33-yarder that set up Seattle's first touchdown.

Right newspaper page (Section E, Tuesday, April 4, 1995):

Today's best bet
Pro basketball,
Seattle at Utah,
Channel 11, 6 p.m.
Complete listings E 2

SPORTS

Bo says goodbye
Bo Jackson, a two-sport star who came back to play baseball after a hip replacement, is retiring at 32. E 4

Seahawks
Signing of Proehl gives Erickson hope for shored-up offense
E 5

 Gill granted medical leave
E 3

Mariners
Talks with Varitek on again; team may make final attempt
E 4

 THE FINAL FOUR

UCLA dunks its demons

O'Bannon's full circle ends at title

BY BUD WITHERS
Seattle Times staff reporter

Bruins' Bailey shows no fear, buries the past

BLAINE NEWNHAM
Times staff columnist

Inside
• Bruins hail injured Tyus Edney as 'real MVP' E 7.
• Taking down championship net 'pinnacle' for UCLA Coach Jim Harrick. E 10.

Toby Bailey's dunk slams the door on Arkansas' hopes of a repeat title. The UCLA freshman had 26 points and nine rebounds.

Dollar fills bill when UCLA appears broke

STEVE KELLEY
Times staff columnist

Richardson isn't saying yet if he'll precede Hogs to NBA

Nucleus of team could to turn pro; reports swirl around coach

BY TOM FARREY
Seattle Times staff reporter

Arkansas' Corliss Williamson, far right, hugs a teammate in the losing locker room.

Silver

The Scotsman

Edinburgh, Scotland

Ally Palmer, Art Director; Terry Watson, Design Editor; Paul Dodds, Photo Editor; Henry Smith, Sports Editor; Keith Anderson, Deputy Sports Editor

Award of Excellence
Asbury Park Press
Neptune, NJ
Harris Siegel, ME/Design & Photography; Andrew Prendimano, Art & Photo Director; Janet L. Michaud, Designer; Celeste LaBrosee, Night Photo Editor; John Quinn, ME/Sports

Award of Excellence
Centre Daily Times
State College, PA
Pat Little, Photographer; Nathan Hockley, Photographer; Deborah Withey, Art Director/Redesign

Gold
• Also Gold for Informational Graphics
The New York Times
New York, NY
Joe Zeff, Designer; Dylan Loeb McClain, Graphics; Patrick J. Lyons, Graphics

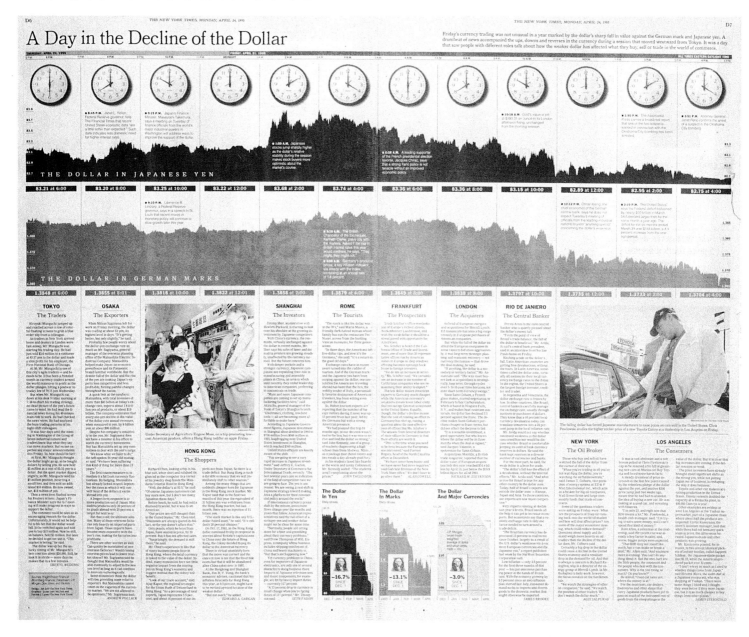

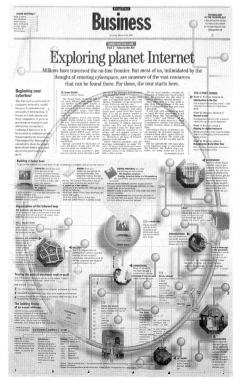

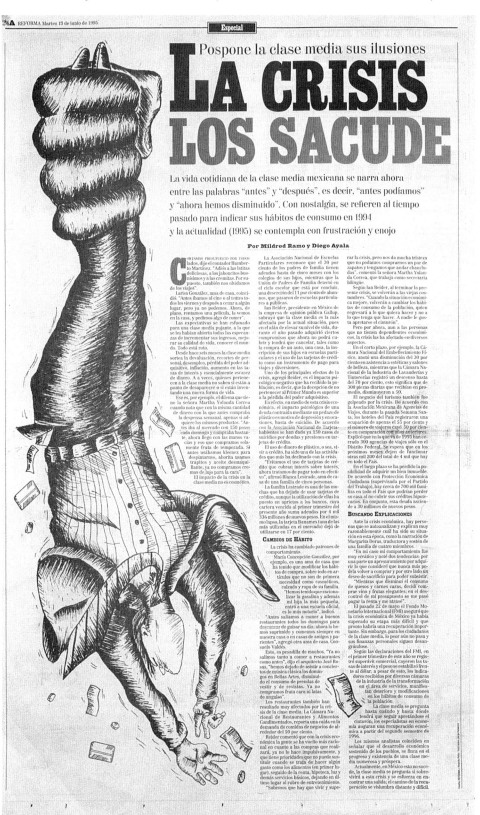

Award of Excellence
Democrat and Chronicle
Rochester, NY
Heather Erwin, Assistant Graphics Editor

Award of Excellence
Democrat and Chronicle
Rochester, NY
Heather Erwin, Assistant Graphics Editor

Award of Excellence
Expansion
Madrid, Spain
Jose Juan Gámez, Design Director; Pablo Ma Ramírez,
Artist & Designer

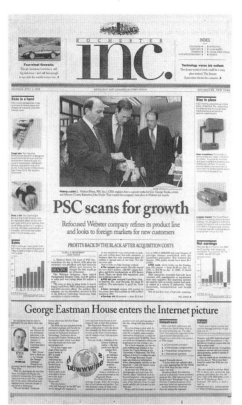

Award of Excellence
Expansion
Madrid, Spain
José Juan Gámez, Design Director; Pablo Ma Ramírez, Designer & Artist; Mar Domingo,
Artist; Blanca Serrano, Artist

Award of Excellence
Expansion
Madrid, Spain
Jose Juan Gamez, Design Director; Pablo Ma Ramirez, Graphic Artist; Antonio Martin
Hervas, Graphic Artist; Mar Domingo, Graphic Artist

Award of Excellence
The Home News
East Brunswick, NJ
Linda Heyniger, Designer; Harris Siegel, ME/Design &
Photography; Teresa Klink, ME/News; Phil Hartman,
Business Editor; Tom Kerr, Art Director

Award of Excellence
The Home News
East Brunswick, NJ
Linda Heyniger, Designer; Harris Siegel, ME/Design &
Photography; Teresa Klink, ME/News; Phil Hartman,
Business Editor; Tom Kerr, Art Director

Award of Excellence
La Gaceta
San Miguel de Tucuman, Argentina
Sergio Fernandez, Art Director & Designer; Mario Garcia,
Design Consultant; Ruben Falci, Designer

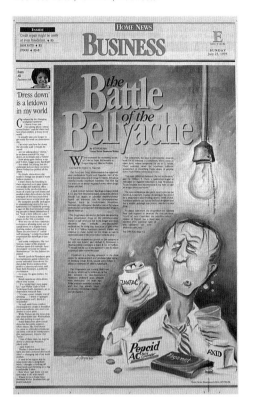

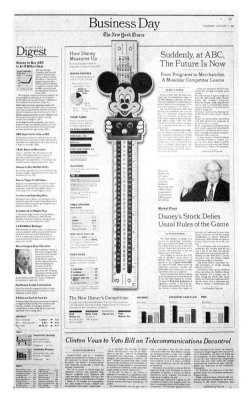

Award of Excellence
• Also Award of Excellence for News Portfolio
The New York Times
New York, NY
Joe Zeff, Designer; Kris Goodfellow, Graphics Editor

Award of Excellence
The New York Times
New York, NY
Ken Brown, Designer

Award of Excellence
The Miami Herald
Miami, FL
Ana Lense-Larrauri, Graphic Artist; Jim Watters, Business
Editor; Randy Stano, Director Editorial Art & Design

Award of Excellence
The Oregonian
Portland, OR
Kirk Christ, Designer; Michael Mode, Artist; Dave Cutler, Artist; Michelle Wise, Art Director

Award of Excellence
Reforma
Mexico City, Mexico
Marcela Burgueño Aburto, Eduardo Danilo, Design; José Luis Barros, Illustrator; Diego Treviño, Photo; René Sánchez, Editor; Ernesto Carrillo, Arturo Jiménez, Graphics Editors; Emilio Deheza, Art Director

Award of Excellence
Richmond Times-Dispatch
Richmond, VA
Stephen Rountree, Artist

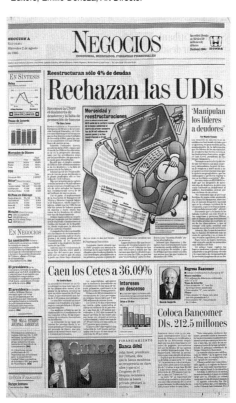

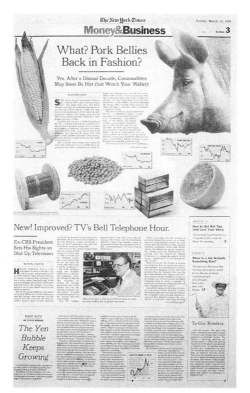

Award of Excellence
San Francisco Examiner
San Francisco, CA
Kelly Frankeny, AME; KT Rabin, Business Editor; Business Staff Mike Gray, Assistant Business Editor; Don Asmussen, Artist

Award of Excellence
The New York Times
New York, NY
Fred Norgaard, Art Director; Dylan McClain, Graphics; Anne Cronin, Graphics

Award of Excellence
The Scotsman
Edinburgh, Scotland
Ally Palmer, Art Director; Terry Watson, Design Editor;
Colin MacKinnon, Business Production Editor; Staff

Silver
Chicago Tribune
Chicago, IL
Andrew Skwish, Art Director; David Syrek, Assistant Design Director

Silver

Reforma

México City, Mexico

Marco Antonio Román, Designer; José Manuel Mendoza, Section Designer; Marissa Macías, Editor; Emilio Deheza, Art Director; Eduardo Danilo, Design Consultant; Arturo Jiménez, Graphics Editor

Silver

The Ball State Daily News

Muncie, IN

Bill Webster, ME Graphics; Al Kraft, Graphics Reporter

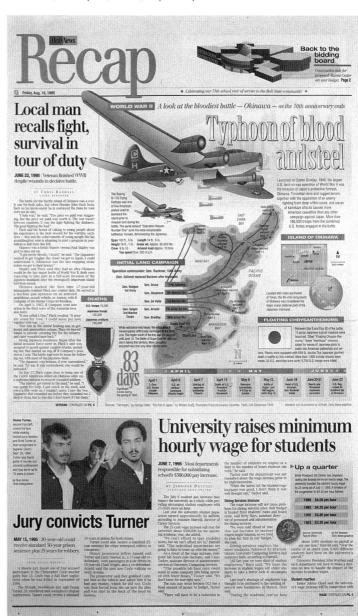

Silver
The Greenville News
Greenville, SC
Channon Seifert, Art Director
& Designer; Wayne Roper,
Editor

Award of Excellence
Reforma
México City, Mexico
José Manuel Mendoza, Section Designer; Marco Antonio
Román, Designer; Israel Mejia, Illustrator; Emilio Deheza,
Art Director; Arturo Jiménez, Graphics Editor; Eduardo
Danilo, Design Consultant

Award of Excellence
Reforma
México City, Mexico
Carlos Guimaraes, Editor; Arturo Jiménez, Graphics Editor;
Alejo Najera, Section Designer; Emilio Deheza, Art
Director; Eduardo Danilo, Design Consultant

Award of Excellence
The New York Times
New York, NY
Greg Ryan, Art Director

Gold
• Also Silver for Photojournalism
Diario de Noticias
Huarte-Pamplona, Spain
Emilio Zazu, Photographer;
Javier Errea, Art Director; Staff

Award of Excellence
Asbury Park Press
Neptune, NJ
Staff; Harris Siegel, ME Design & Photography; Andrew
Prendimano, Art & Photo Director, Designer

Award of Excellence
• Also Award of Excellence for Photojournalism
The Detroit News
Detroit, MI
Dale Peskin, DME; Joe Gray, Assistant News Editor; Bob
Howard, Page Designer; Charles Tines, Photographer

Award of Excellence
The Orange County Register
Santa Ana, CA
John Fabris, Design Team Leader; Nanette Bisher,
AME/Art Director; Staff

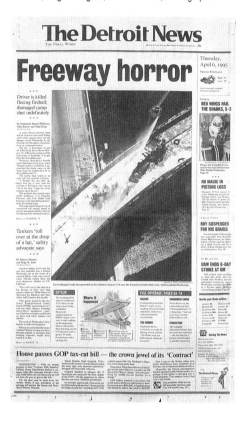

Award of Excellence
Chicago Tribune
Chicago, IL
Staff

Award of Excellence
Diario 16
Madrid, Spain
Juan Varela, Art Director; Staff

Award of Excellence
The Oregonian
Portland, OR
Staff

Award of Excellence
Saint Paul Pioneer Press
St. Paul, MN
Joe Sevick, News Editor; Kirk Lyttle, Graphic Artist; Andy King, Photographer

Award of Excellence
The Times-Picayune
New Orleans, LA
George Berke, Photographer; Doug Parker, Photo Editor; Paula Devila, News Editor; Photo Staff

Award of Excellence
San Francisco Examiner
San Francisco, CA
Kelly Frankeny, AME Design; Mignon Khargie, Designer; Don Asmussen, Art; Richard Paoli, Photo Director; K.T. Rabin, Business Ed.; Jay Johnson, Exec. NE; Marjorie Rice, Graphics Ed.; Heidi Benson, Style Ed.

Award of Excellence
The Virginian-Pilot
Norfolk, VA
Buddy Moore, Designer; Alex Burrows, Photo Editor; Bill Tiernan, Photographer; Paul Aiken, Photographer; Bob Voros, Artist

Award of Excellence
Colorado Springs Gazette Telegraph
Colorado Springs, CO
Trich Redman, Art Director & Designer; Dan Cotter, Designer; Terri Fleming, DME

Award of Excellence
The Dallas Morning News
Dallas, TX
Staff

The Dallas Morning News

Terror
Oklahoma City car bomb kills at least 31

Children ensnared in attack

Scores missing in rubble of office building

Scenes of carnage bring horror to the heartland

Dazed family members gather at church to await word on kin

Silver
The Virginian-Pilot
Norfolk, VA

Buddy Moore, Designer; Latane Jones, Designer; Tracy Porter, Designer; Eric Seidman, Art Director; Alex Burrows, Photo Editor; Julie Elman, Photo Editor; Tom Warhover, Editor

The Virginian-Pilot

WEDNESDAY OCTOBER 4, 1995

50¢ · SERVING SOUTHEASTERN VIRGINIA AND NORTHEASTERN NORTH CAROLINA · 130th Year, No. 233

A FREE MAN

O.J. Simpson
"This part of the incredible nightmare . . . is over."

Fred Goldman, father of victim Ronald Goldman
"Last June 13th, '94, was the worst nightmare of my life. This is the second."

Gil Garcetti, Los Angeles district attorney
"THEIR DECISION WAS BASED ON EMOTION; THAT OVERCAME THE REASON."

Brenda Moran, juror
"I think we did the right thing – in fact I know we did."

ASSOCIATED PRESS
As the verdict is read, emotions pour out: from the sadness of Ronald Goldman's sister Kim and father, Fred, at left, to the jubilation of O.J. Simpson, center, and his mother, Eunice.

Orenthal James Simpson was freed Tuesday of charges that he murdered his ex-wife, Nicole Brown Simpson, and her friend Ronald Goldman, but the verdict has not freed a nation to whom his trial became a lengthy, painful sounding of the deep divisions among us.

ANALYSIS
BY DAVE ADDIS
STAFF WRITER

ASSOCIATED PRESS
At New York City's Rockefeller Center, a crowd gathers at the window of the NBC-TV News street-level studio for the live broadcast of the verdict Tuesday.

O.J. returns home, leaving nation with doubt, division

FROM WIRE REPORTS

LOS ANGELES — Bringing one of history's most riveting courtroom dramas to a climax, O.J. Simpson was acquitted of two counts of murder Tuesday, verdicts that set the football Hall of Fame athlete free 474 days after he was arrested and charged with a brutal double-homicide.

Please see Simpson, Page A14

MORE TRIAL COVERAGE INSIDE TODAY'S PILOT

Justice	Relations	Day 372	Aftermath	Obsession	Images	Comment
A6	A7	A8	A9	A10	A11	A12

Award of Excellence
The Detroit News
Detroit, MI
Dale Peskin, DME; Chris Kozlowski, Design Editor; Chris Willis, David Kordalski, Asst. Graphics Editors; Shayne Bowman, Asst. Design Editor; Joe Gray, Asst. News Editor; Theresa Badovich, Page Designer; Tim Summers, Graphic Artist

★ EXTRA ★
The Detroit News

O.J.'S FREE
★ ★ ★
Simpson smiles, waves to jury as verdict's announced

BREAKING NEWS
1st Degree Murder: Not Guilty

INSIDE THIS SECTION

Award of Excellence
The New York Times
New York, NY
Tom Bodkin, Associate ME & Design Director; Staff

Award of Excellence
• Also Award of Excellence for Informational Graphics
The Oregonian
Portland, OR
Murray Koodish, Designer; Michelle Wise, Graphics Director; Galen Barnett, News Design Editor; Staff, Artists

Award of Excellence
Savannah News-Press
Savannah, GA
Sharilyn Hufford, News Designer; Claudia E. Ortega, Features/Sports Planning Editor; Dan Suwyn, ME

Award of Excellence
The Seattle Times
Seattle, WA
Karen Klinkenberg, News Designer; David Miller, Art Director

Award of Excellence
The St. Petersburg Times
St. Petersburg, FL
Staff

Award of Excellence
The Virginian-Pilot
Norfolk, VA
Bob Fleming, Designer; Latane Jones, Designer; Bob Lynn, AME Graphics; Eric Seidman, Art Director; Alex Burrows, Photo Editor; Julie Elman, Photo Editor; Brian Stallcop, News Editor; Bob Voros, Artist

Award of Excellence
The Washington Times
Washington, DC
Joseph W. Scopin, AME Graphics; Greg Groesch, Art Director & Designer; Geoffrey Etnyre, News Editor; Brian Sink, Asst News Editor; Glen Stubbe, Director of Photography

Award of Excellence
The Washington Times
Washington, DC
Joseph W. Scopin, AME Graphics; Greg Groesch, Art Director & Designer; Geoffrey Etnyre, News Editor; Brian Sink, Asst. News Editor; Glen Stubbe, Photo Director; Steven Katz, Asst. News Editor

Award of Excellence
Chicago Tribune
Chicago, IL
Staff

Award of Excellence
The Detroit News
Detroit, MI
Dale Peskin, DME; Joe Gray, Assistant News Editor; Bob Howard, Page Designer

Award of Excellence
San Jose Mercury News
San Jose, CA
Mike Mayer, News Editor; Bryan Monroe, AME Graphics; Scott Demuesy, Photo Editor

Award of Excellence
The Seattle Times
Seattle, WA
Bo Hok Cline, News Graphic Designer; David Miller, Art Director & Designer; Michael Kellams, Designer; Fred Nelson, Photo Editor

Silver

Saint Paul Pioneer Press

St. Paul, MN

Peter Weinberger, Visuals Editor; Lauri Treston, Deputy VE Design; Joanne Ostendorf, Deputy VE Graphics; David Hardman, Graphic Artist; Jean Pieri, Photographer

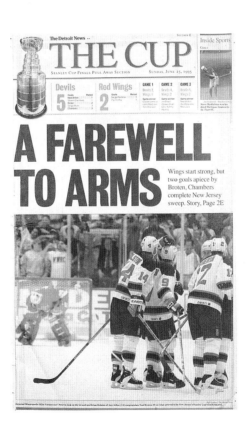

Silver
Diario de Noticias
Huarte-Pamplona, Spain
Carlos Garcia, Assistant
Art Director; Javier Errea,
Art Director; Elena Sanz,
Designer; Tita Lorenz,
Designer

Award of Excellence
The Orange County Register
Santa Ana, CA
Nanette Bisher, AME/Art Director; Ken Brusic, Executive
Editor; Tonnie Katz, Editor; Staff

Award of Excellence
The Seattle Times
Seattle, WA
Celeste Ericsson, Christine Cox, Designers; Karen Kerche-
lich, Graphics Ed.; Randee Fox, Paul Schmid, Artists; Bill
Dietrich, Photo; Fred Nelson, Photo Ed.; David Miller, Art Dir.

Award of Excellence
The Seattle Times
Seattle, WA
Bo Hok Cline, News Artist; David Miller, Art Director; Liz
McClure, Asst. Art Director; Karen Klinkenberg, News
Designer; Alan Berner, Jimi Lott, Photographers; Staff

Award of Excellence
The Orange County Register
Santa Ana, CA
Nanette Bisher, AME/Art Director; Ken Brusic, Executive
Editor; Tonnie Katz, Editor; Bill Cunningham, Wire Editor;
Bernadette Finley, Senior Designer; John Fabris, Design
Team Leader; David Medzerian, Design Team Leader;
Turney George, Graphics Editor; Staff

Award of Excellence
Star Tribune
Minneapolis, MN
Greg Branson, Graphic Artist/Designer; Terry Sauer,
Designer; Tim Campbell, Graphics Editor; Roger Buoen,
National Editor; Bill Dunn, Design Director; Steve Ronald,
DME

Award of Excellence
Chicago Tribune
Chicago, IL
Tribune Staff

Award of Excellence
The Daily Times-Call
Longmont, CO
Christopher Anderson, Photographer

Award of Excellence
Saint Paul Pioneer Press
St Paul, MN
Peter Weinberger, Visuals Editor; Lauri Treston, Deputy
VE Design; Joanne Ostendorf, Deputy VE Graphics; Scott
Takushi, Photographer; Alex Leary, Graphic Artist; Tim
Montgomery, Graphic Artist; David Hardman, Graphic
Artist

Award of Excellence
Saint Paul Pioneer Press
St Paul, MN
Peter Weinberger, Visuals Editor; Lauri Treston, Deputy
VE Design; Joanne Ostendorf, Deputy VE Graphics;
Richard Marshall, Deputy VE Photo; David Hardman,
Graphic Artist

3

Regularly appearing section winners were selected after reviewing three issues. Circulation size was taken into consideration. Pages could include opinion, lifestyle/features, entertainment, food, fashion, home/real estate, travel, science/technology or any other feature page selected by the staff.

Features

- Regularly Appearing Sections
- Page Design

Award of Excellence
The Scotsman
Edinburgh, Scotland
Ally Palmer, Art Director; Terry Watson, Design Editor; Kenny Kemp, Chief Features Sub-Editor; Staff

Award of Excellence
The Boston Globe
Boston, MA
Lucy Batholomay, Designer & AME Design; Chris Chinlund, Editor

Award of Excellence
Folha de S. Paulo
São Paulo, Brazil
Alcino Leite, Editor; Cassio Starling, Deputy Editor; Renata Buono, Page Design

·· Göteborgs-Posten
SÖNDAG 3

ODUBBAT ÄR BÄST?
Louis de Funes, den energiske
franske skådespelaren, säg vi i
Den lille badaren förra söndagen.
Många tittare har hört av sig till
TV-linjen och är upprörda över att
filmen var dubbad på engelska.
TV, sidan 74

TONSPRÅK SOM BERÖR
Anna-Lotta Larsson har till sitt
nya album valt sånger med tonspråk som berör och texter som
kan väcka något inom lyssna-
ren; minnen, tankar, värdering-
ar.
Nöjet, sidan 70

KULTUR	60
SÖNDAG	62
NÖJE	70
RADIO & TV	73
NÖJES- ANNONSER	71

27 AUGUSTI 1995

Vit clown.

FOTO: HANS GEDDA

CIRKUSLIV

En närbild av cirkuslivet. Clownens
ansikte speglar allt det som ryms i or-
det cirkus. Fotografen heter Hans
Gedda. Berömd för sina inträngande
människoporträtt. Förra året kunde man se hans cirkusbilder
i manegen hos Cirkus Scott. Nu har de samlats i en bok.
Fotografins Nils Ferlin ger oss en del av
cirkusens hemligheter – och poesi.
SIDAN 63

Gasket Case

During her 14-year marriage
to an auto-parts mogul,
Denise Hrudka lived in the lap of luxury.
Then her husband stood up.

BY LISA DAVIS

Award of Excellence
The Albuquerque Tribune
Albuquerque, NM
Joan Carlin, Designer

Award of Excellence
Anchorage Daily News
Anchorage, AK
Dee Boyles, Illustrator & Designer; Galie Jean-Louis,
Features Design Director

Award of Excellence
Anchorage Daily News
Anchorage, AK
Lance Lekander, Illustrator & Designer; Galie Jean-Louis,
Features Design Director

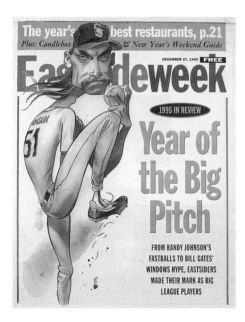

Award of Excellence
Eastsideweek
Seattle, WA
Barbara Dow, Art Director & Designer; John Kascht,
Illustrator

Award of Excellence
Göteborgs-Posten
Goteborg, Sweden
Tomas Karlsson, Illustrator; Eleonor Ekström-Frisk,
Designer

Award of Excellence
Göteborgs-Posten
Goteborg, Sweden
Karin Teghammar Arell, Designer; Peter Claesson,
Photographer

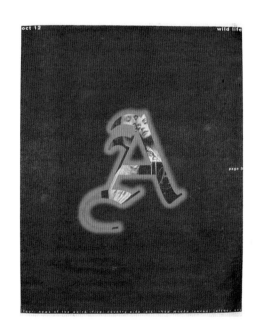

Silver
The Albuquerque Tribune
Albuquerque, NM
Jeff Neumann, Designer

Award of Excellence
The Washington Times
Washington, DC
Joseph W. Scopin, AME Graphics; Jennifer Pritchard, Art Director & Designer

Award of Excellence
The Virginian-Pilot
Norfolk, VA
Sam Hundley, Designer; Denis Finley, Editor; David
Simpson, Copy Editor

Award of Excellence
The Albuquerque Tribune
Albuquerque, NM
Jeff Neumann, Designer

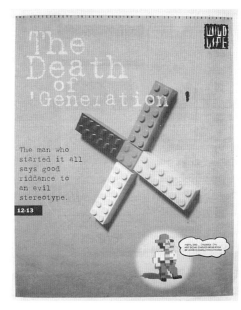

Award of Excellence
The Boston Globe
Boston, MA
Aldona Charlton, Art Director & Designer; Lane Turner,
Photographer; Jan Shepherd, Editor; Shirley Newsom,
Copy & Makeup

Award of Excellence
Dayton Daily News
Dayton, OH
Randy Palmer, Designer; Ty Greenlees, Photographer;
Lee Waigand, Art Director; John Thomson, AME Graphics;
James Lloyd, Section Editor

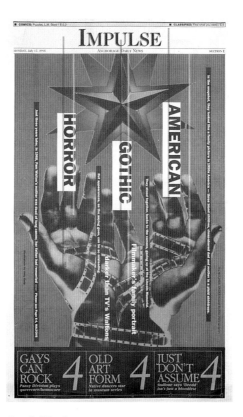

Award of Excellence
Anchorage Daily News
Anchorage, AK
Amy Guip, Photographer; Galie Jean-Louis, Designer &
Features Design Director

Award of Excellence
Anchorage Daily News
Anchorage, AK
Dee Boyles, Designer; Galie Jean-Louis, Features Design
Director; Johnny Buzzario, Photographer

Award of Excellence
Jacksonville Journal-Courier
Jacksonville, IL
Mike Miner, Editor/Designer; Steve Copper,
Editor/Designer

Award of Excellence
Le Devoir
Montreal, Canada
Roland-Yves Carignan, Page Designer; Michel Belair,
Section Editor; Benoit Munger, Copy Editor; Roland-Yves
Carignan, Deputy Editor-in-Chief/Art Director

Award of Excellence
Le Devoir
Montreal, Canada
Roland-Yves Carignan, Page Designer; Michel Belair,
Section Editor; Benoit Munger, Copy Editor; Roland-Yves
Carignan, Deputy Editor-in-Chief/Art Director

Award of Excellence
Centre Daily Times
State College, PA
Jana Smedley, Designer; Deborah Withey, Art Director/Designer

Award of Excellence
Le Devoir
Montreal, Canada
Roland-Yves Carignan, Page Designer; Michel Belair,
Section Editor; Roland-Yves Carignan, Deputy Editor-in-
Chief/Art Director

Award of Excellence
Le Devoir
Montreal, Canada
Roland-Yves Carignan, Page Designer, Deputy Editor &
Art Director; Michel Bélair, Section Editor

Award of Excellence
The San Diego Union-Tribune
San Diego, CA
Amy Stirnkorb, Designer

Award of Excellence
NRC Handelsblad
Rotterdam, Netherlands
Kees Endenburg, Design Editor; Berry van Gerwen,
Illustrator

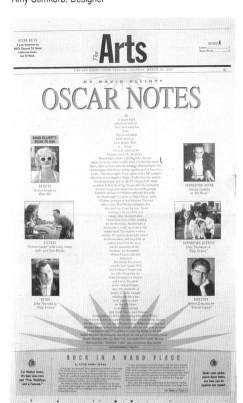

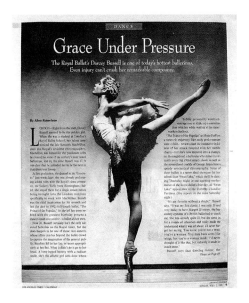

Award of Excellence
Los Angeles Times
Los Angeles, CA
Diana Shantic, Art Director

Award of Excellence
San Jose Mercury News
San Jose, CA
Nuri J. Ducassi, Features Design Director; Martin Gee,
Designer

Award of Excellence
The Seattle Times
Seattle, WA
Chuck Eichten, Designer & Writer; Jan Even, Editor; David
Miller, Art Director

Silver
El País de las Tentaciones
Madrid, Spain
Nuria Muiña, Designer;
Wladimir Marnich, Designer;
Ignacio Rubio, Designer;
Miguel Gener, Photo Editor;
Vicente Jiménez, Editor;
Fernando Gutiérrez, Designer

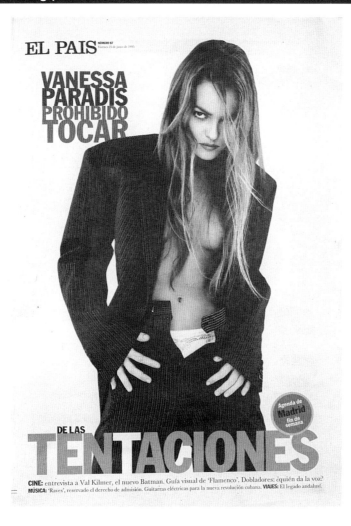

Award of Excellence
The Virginian-Pilot
Norfolk, VA
Sam Hundley, Designer; Roberta Vowell, Editor

Award of Excellence
• Also Award of Excellence for Features Portfolio
The Virginian-Pilot
Norfolk, VA
Sam Hundley, Designer; Roberta Vowell, Editor

Silver
Le Devoir
Montreal, Canada
Roland-Yves Carignan,
Deputy Editor-in-Chief/Art
Director; Michel Bélair,
Section Editor; Yves
D'Avignon, Copy Editor;
Benoît Munger, Copy Editor

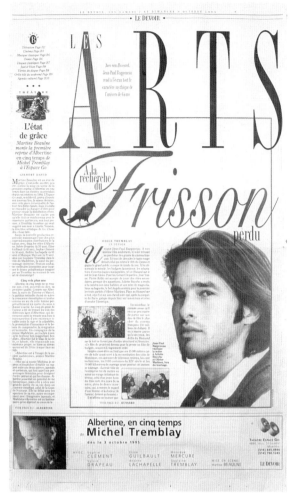

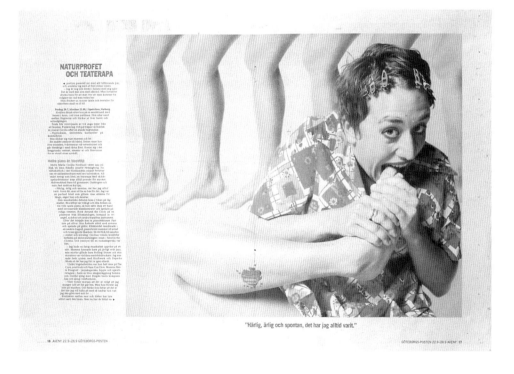

Award of Excellence
Göteborgs-Posten
Goteborg, Sweden
Karina Hansson, Designer; Henrik Strömberg, Designer; Lena Strömberg, Designer; Per Wahlberg, Photographer

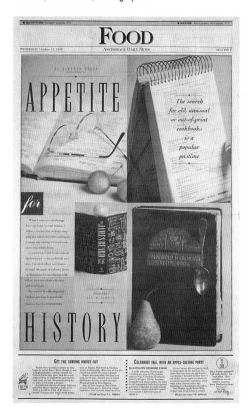

El Nuevo Herald

Miami, FL

Aurora Arrue, Illustrator & Designer; Angela Swafford, Food Editor; Herman Vega, Director of Editorial Art & Design

Award of Excellence

El Norte

Monterrey, Mexico

Maurico Gutiérrez, Designer; Juan José Cerón, Photographer; Alejandra García, Photo-Artist; Raúl Braulio Martinez, Art Director; Carmen A. Escobedo, Graphics Editor; Alragracia Fuentes, Editor

Award of Excellence

San Francisco Examiner

San Francisco, CA

Kelly Frankeny, AME Design; Mignon Khargie, Illustrator & Designer; Lynn Forbes, Epicure Editor

Award of Excellence

San Francisco Examiner

San Francisco, CA

Kelly Frankeny, AME Design; Mignon Khargie, Illustrator & Designer; Jo Mancuso, Epicure Editor

Award of Excellence

San Francisco Examiner

San Francisco, CA

Kelly Frankeny, AME Design; Mignon Khargie, Illustrator & Designer; Jo Mancuso, Epicure Editor

Award of Excellence

San Francisco Examiner

San Francisco, CA

Kelly Frankeny, AME Design; Don McCartney, Designer; Jo Mancuso, Epicure Editor; Don Asmussen, Artist

Award of Excellence
San Jose Mercury News
San Jose, CA
David Frazier, Page Designer

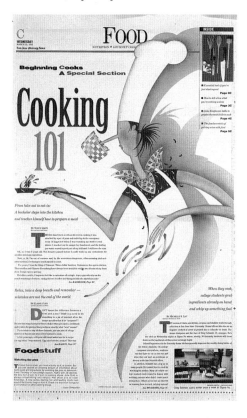

Award of Excellence
The Star-Ledger
Newark, NJ
Mark Morrissey, Designer; Chris Buckley, Art Director;
Linda Fowler, Section Editor; Ed Bishop,
Photographer/Envision

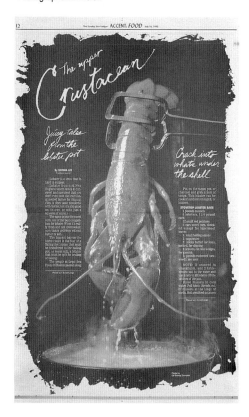

Award of Excellence
The Virginian-Pilot
Norfolk, VA
Peter Dishal, Designer; Christopher Reddick,
Photographer; Alex Burrows, Photographer; Pat Dooley,
Editor

Award of Excellence
The Budapest Sun
Budapest, Hungary
Craig Snelgrove, Designer; Reuben Stern, Art Director

Award of Excellence
AM De Leon
Leon, Mexico
Beatriz Zambrano, Art Director; Luis Estrada, Designer;
Sebastian Martinez, Photographer

Award of Excellence
El Norte
Monterrey, Mexico
Lourdes De la Rosa, Designer; Juan José Cerón,
Photographer; Yamil López y Arturo Rangel, Photo-Artist;
Raúl Braulio Martinez, Art Director; Carmen A. Escobedo,
Graphics Editor

Award of Excellence
El Nuevo Herald
Miami, FL
José Pacheco Silva, Designer; Blanca Silva, Editor

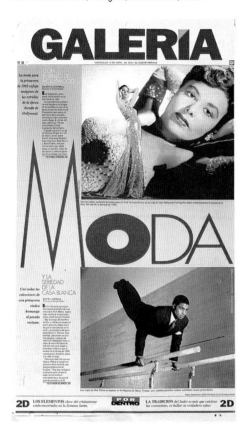

Award of Excellence
El Norte
Monterrey, Mexico
Lourdes De la Rosa, Designer; Estudio El Norte ,
Photographer; Carmen A. Escobedo, Graphics Editor;
Raúl Braulio Martinez, Art Director

Award of Excellence
Göteborgs-Posten
Goteborg, Sweden
Dawel Flato, Photographer; Gunilla Wernhamn, Designer

Award of Excellence
Diario de Noticias
Huarte-Pamplona, Spain
Javier Errea, Designer

Award of Excellence
Morgenavisen Jyllands-Posten
Viby, Denmark
Ole Gravesen, Designer

Award of Excellence
The News & Observer
Raleigh, NC
Sherry Carwell, Designer; Kate Anthony, Design Director/Features; Roger Winstead, Photographer; David Pickel, Presentation/Design Editor

Award of Excellence
The Dallas Morning News
Dallas, TX
Peggy Cox-Reynolds, Designer/Illustrator; Laura Betts, Designer; Evans Caglage, Photographer; Tammy Theis, Fashion Stylist; Paula Nelson, Photographer

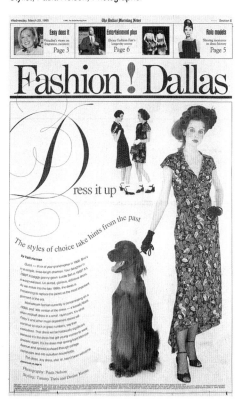

Award of Excellence
The Home News
East Brunswick, NJ
Mary Clark Ladd, Designer; Harris Siegel, ME/Design & Photography; Teresa Klink, ME/News; Mary Price, Section Editor; Tom Kerr, Art Director

Award of Excellence
San Francisco Examiner
San Francisco, CA
Kelly Frankeny, AME Design; Mignon Khargie, Designer; Jo Mancuso, Habitat Editor

Award of Excellence
San Francisco Examiner
San Francisco, CA
Kelly Frankeny, AME Design; Mignon Khargie, Designer; Jo Mancuso, Habitat Editor

Award of Excellence
Detroit Free Press
Detroit, MI
James Denk, Designer; Allison Young, Photographer

Award of Excellence
The New York Times
New York, NY
Nicki Kalish, Art Director

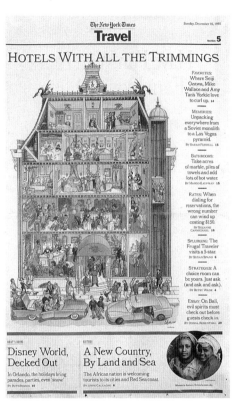

Award of Excellence
The New York Times
New York, NY
Nicki Kalish, Art Director

Award of Excellence
The News & Observer
Raleigh, NC
Brenda Konopka, Designer; Kate Anthony, Design
Director/Features; David Pickel, Presentation/Design
Editor

Award of Excellence
San Francisco Examiner
San Francisco, CA
Kelly Frankeny, AME Design; Don McCartney, Designer;
Don George, Travel Editor

Award of Excellence
● Also Award of Excellence for Illustration
San Francisco Examiner
San Francisco, CA
Kelly Frankeny, AME Design; Don George, Travel Editor;
Mignon Khargie, Designer/Illustrator

Award of Excellence
San Francisco Examiner
San Francisco, CA
Kelly Frankeny, AME Design; Mignon Khargie,
Designer/Illustrator; Don George, Travel Editor

Award of Excellence
• Also Award of Excellence for Illustration
San Francisco Examiner
San Francisco, CA
Kelly Frankeny, AME Design; Mignon Khargie,
Designer/Illustrator; Don George, Travel Editor

Award of Excellence
The Boston Globe
Boston, MA
Cindy Daniels, Art Director; Sean McNaughton,
Informational Graphic Designer

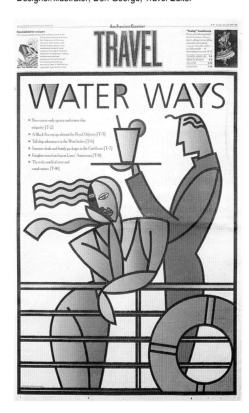

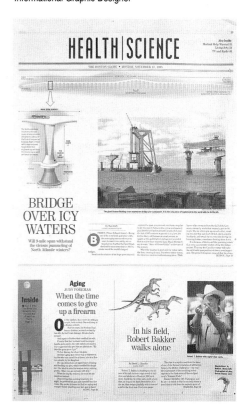

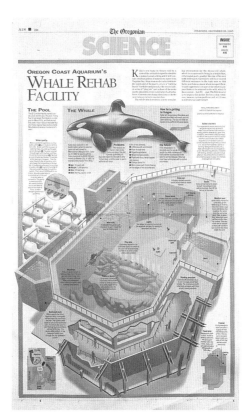

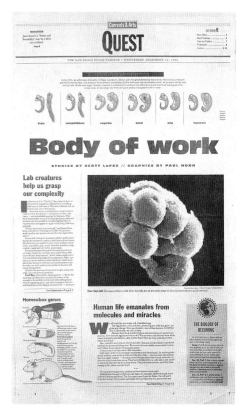

Award of Excellence
The Hartford Courant
Hartford, CT
Chris Moore, Designer & Illustrator; Christian Potter Drury,
Art Director

Award of Excellence
• Also Award of Excellence for Informational Graphics
The Oregonian
Portland, OR
Steve Cowden, Artist & Researcher; Michelle Wise,
Graphics Director

Award of Excellence
The San Diego Union-Tribune
San Diego, CA
Amy Stirnkorb, Designer; Paul Horn, Graphics Journalist

Award of Excellence
Anchorage Daily News
Anchorage, AK
Lance Lekander, Designer; Galie Jean-Louis,
Features Design Director

Award of Excellence
Anchorage Daily News
Anchorage, AK
Kevin Ellis, Designer; Galie Jean-Louis, Features
Design Editor; Barry Blitt, Illustrator

Award of Excellence
Anchorage Daily News
Anchorage, AK
Kevin Ellis, Designer; Galie Jean-Louis, Features
Design Editor; Erik Hill, Photographer

Award of Excellence
El Norte
Monterrey, Mexico
Carmen T. Chacón, Designer & Photo-Artist; Arturo López, Photographer; Marcela Amaya,
Graphics Editor; Raúl Braulio Martinez, Art Director

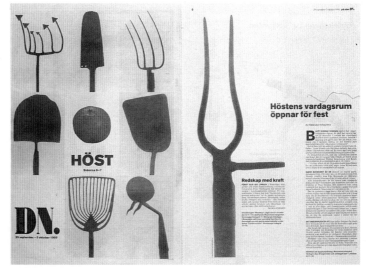

Award of Excellence
Dagens Nyheter
Stockholm, Sweden
Lotten Ekman, Designer; Peder Björkegren, Photographer; Nina Ericson, Photographer

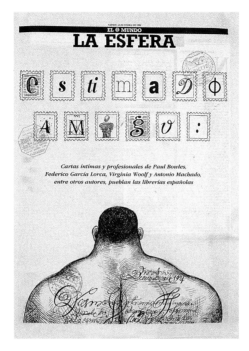

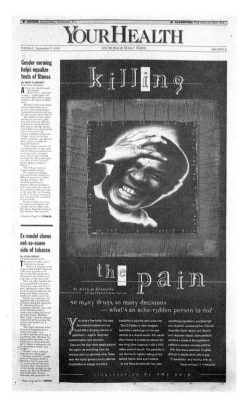

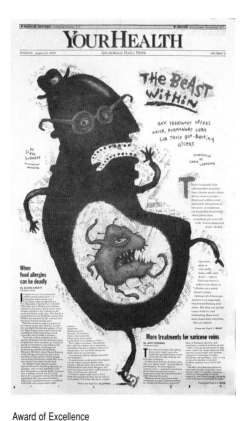

Award of Excellence
The Home News
East Brunswick, NJ
Kathleen Dzielak, Section Editor; Harris Siegel, ME/Design
& Photography, Designer; Stefan Martin, Illustrator; Tom
Kerr, Art Director

Award of Excellence
Göteborgs-Posten
Goteborg, Sweden
Karin Teghammar Arell, Designer; Helené Furness,
Photographer

Award of Excellence
Helsingborgs Dagblad
Helsingborg, Sweden
Eva Engwall, Design Editor; Zarah Lüsch, Design Editor

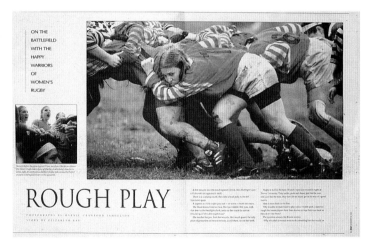

Award of Excellence
Providence Journal-Bulletin
Providence, RI
Debra Page-Trim, Designer; Mick Cochran, Art Direction/Designer; Marnie Crawford
Samuelson, Photographer; Anestis Diakopoulos, Picture Editor

Award of Excellence
Göteborgs-Posten
Goteborg, Sweden
Gunilla Wernhamn, Designer; Sofia Sabel, Photographer

Award of Excellence

Baltimore Jewish Times

Baltimore, MD

Joel Rodgers, Illustrator; Robyn Katz, Art Director

Award of Excellence

La Gaceta

San Miguel de Tucuman, Argentina

Sergio Fernandez, Art Director & Designer; Mario Garcia, Design Consultant; Oscar Ferronato, Designer

Award of Excellence

Diario 16

Madrid, Spain

Juan Varela, Art Director; Staff

Magazines had to be distributed with a newspaper to qualify for this category. Magazines could enter the Special Section category if the sections appeared fewer than four times a year. Covers were judged in two divisions: black & white and/or one color and two or more colors. Three complete issues of the magazine had to be entered for overall design.

Magazines

- Overall Design
- Special Sections
- Cover Design
- Page Design

Award of Excellence
El Mundo Magazine
Madrid, Spain
Rodrigo Sánchez, Art Director; Miguel Buckenmeyer, Designer; Amparo Redondo, Designer

Award of Excellence
San Francisco Examiner
San Francisco, CA
Joey Rigg, Designer; Zahid Sardar, Designer; Paul Wilner, Examiner Magazine Editor

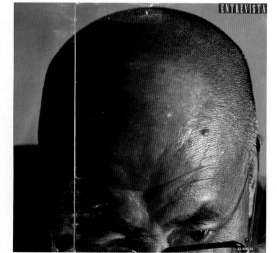

Award of Excellence
El Pais Semanal
Madrid, Spain
Eugenio Gonzalez, Design Director; Isabel Benito, Designer; Gustavo Sanchez, Designer; Mariapaz Domingo, Designer

Silver
El Mundo Magazine
Madrid, Spain
Rodrigo Sánchez, Art Director & Designer; Miguel Buckenmeyer, Designer; Amparo Redondo, Designer

Rodajes

LA EPOPEYA DEL CINE

por Jesús Ferrero

L A FICCIÓN CONVERTIDA EN REALIDAD. ESA FUE LA GRAN QUIMERA CONSEGUIDA POR EL SÉPTIMO ARTE, LA RECREACIÓN HASTA EL INFINITO DE LO POSIBLE Y LO IMPOSIBLE. NACIERON CIUDADES DE CARTÓN PIEDRA, ESCENARIOS ARTIFICIALES DONDE RODAR COMO SI FUERA LA VIDA MISMA. FUE LA GRAN EPOPEYA DEL CINE. AQUELLOS GRANDES RODAJES QUE MOVILIZABAN MILES DE PERSONAS LLEGARON INCLUSO A NUESTRO PAÍS. SE VIERON LOS TRUCOS QUE SE MUEVEN ENTRE BASTIDORES. SE PRODUJERON EXTASIS ANTE LAS GRÚAS, LOS FOCOS, LOS OPERADORES. HOY SE RINDE CULTO AL RECUERDO DE ALGUNOS DE LOS MÁS MEMORABLES RODAJES DE UN SIGLO DE ORO PARA EL ESPECTÁCULO.

fotografías: Kobal Collection

24 MAGAZINE

El Platø

PRÊT-À-PORTER

EL FOTÓGRAFO GUEORGI PINKHASSOV SE INTRODUCE ENTRE BASTIDORES Y MIRA CON SU CÁMARA A LOS QUE SE TRABAJAN PARA DEJARSE VER. ES EL RODAJE DE «PRÊT-À-PORTER», PELÍCULA QUE DEFIENDE SU DIRECTOR, ROBERT ALTMAN, EN ESTA ENTREVISTA

por Marcus Rothe

UNA FICCIÓN DE CARÁCTER SOCIOLÓGICO CON UN DOCUMENTO REAL: LAS PASARELAS DE PARÍS. ALTMAN UTILIZA, UNA VEZ MÁS,

SU DEMOLEDOR MARTILLO DE MITOS: PONE AL DESNUDO LA MODA. VARIAS PELÍCULAS COHABITAN EN UNA: UNA INVESTIGACIÓN PO-

LICIACA DE UN ASESINATO, UN ASUNTO DE CAMA ENTRE DOS PERIODISTAS, UN DRAMA ENTRE MADRE E HIJO... ADEMÁS, UN GRAN

DESFILE DE ACTORES: LAUREN BACALL, KIM BASINGER, JULIA ROBERTS, SOFIA LOREN, MARCELLO MASTROIANNI, TIM ROBBINS...

«LA PELÍCULA NO TRATA DE LOS VESTIDOS, SINO DE LA DESNUDEZ»

fotografías: Gueorgi Pinkhassov

42 MAGAZINE   43 MAGAZINE

Silver
El Mundo Magazine
Madrid, Spain
Rodrigo Sánchez, Art Director & Designer; Carmelo Caderot, Design Director

Award of Excellence
El Mundo Magazine
Madrid, Spain
Rodrigo Sánchez, Art Director & Designer; Miguel Buckenmeyer, Designer; Amparo Redondo, Designer

Award of Excellence
El Mundo Magazine
Madrid, Spain
Rodrigo Sánchez, Art Director & Designer; Miguel Buckenmeyer, Designer; Amparo Redondo, Designer

Award of Excellence
The New York Times Magazine
New York, NY
Janet Froelich, Art Director; Joel Cuyler, Designer;
Sebastião Salgado, Photographer; Kathy Ryan, Photo
Editor

Silver
El Mundo Magazine
Madrid, Spain
Rodrigo Sánchez, Art Director; Miguel Buckenmeyer, Designer; Amparo Redondo, Designer

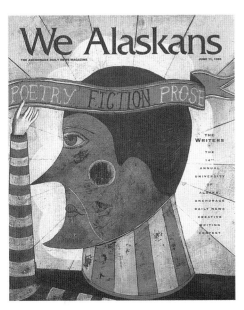

Award of Excellence
• Also Awards of Excellence for Illustration & Magazine Portfolio
Anchorage Daily News
Anchorage, AK
Pamela Dunlap-Shohl, Designer; Christian Northeast,
Illustrator; Galie Jean-Louis, Features Design Director

Gold
El Pais Semanal
Madrid, Spain
David García, Deputy Editor; Eugenio González, Design Director; Isabel Benito, Designer; Gustavo Sanchez, Designer; Mariapaz Domingo, Designer; José M. Navia, Photo Editor; Francis Giacobetti, Photographer

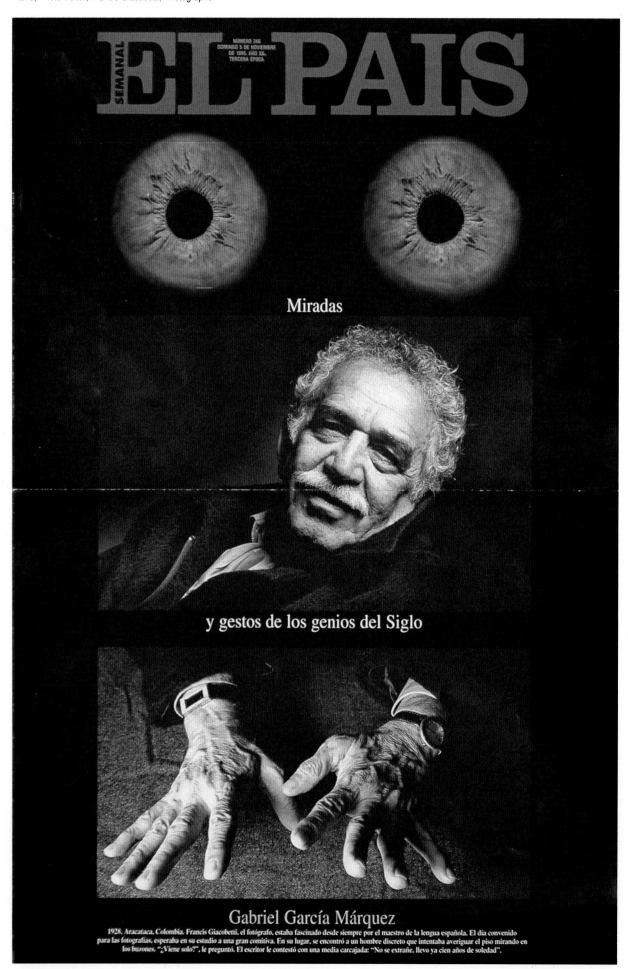

Award of Excellence
El Mundo Magazine
Madrid, Spain
Rodrigo Sánchez, Art Director & Designer; Miguel
Buckenmeyer, Designer; Amparo Redondo, Designer

Award of Excellence
El Mundo Magazine
Madrid, Spain
Rodrigo Sánchez, Art Director & Designer; Miguel
Buckenmeyer, Designer; Amparo Redondo, Designer

Award of Excellence
The Chicago Tribune Magazine
Chicago, IL
Nancy J. Canfield, Creative Director; Denis Gosselin,
Editor; Douglas Balz, ME; Kirt Weed, Art Director; Brenda
Butler, Senior Features Editor; Margaret Carroll, Assistant
Editor; Clarence Petersen, Assistant Editor; Anna Seeto,
Production Assistant; Tom Rosborough, Illustrator

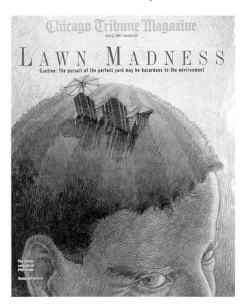

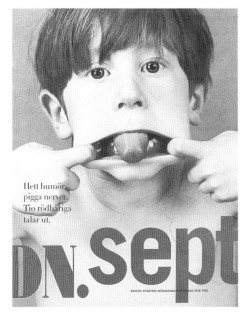

Award of Excellence
Dagens Nyheter
Stockholm, Sweden
Gunilla Eloh, Editor; Susanne Walstrom, Photographer

Award of Excellence
El Pais Semanal
Madrid, Spain
Eugenio Gonzalez, Design Director; Isabel Benito,
Designer; Gustavo Sanchez, Designer; Mariapaz
Domingo, Designer; Jose M. Navia, Picture Editor; Angel
De Pedro, Illustrator; David Garcia, Deputy Editor

Award of Excellence
El Periodico de Catalunya/El Dominical
Barcelona, Spain
Ferran Sendra, Designer; Ricardo Feriche, Creative
Director; Nuria Miquel, Designer; Kim Salomon, Designer;
Alejandro Yofre, Picture Editor; Hector Chimirri, News
Editor; Rafael Nadal, Vice Editor; Jorge Represa,
Photographer

Award of Excellence
The Philadelphia Inquirer Magazine
Philadelphia, PA
Bert Fox, Art Director/Photo Editor/Designer; Christine
Dunleavy, Design Director; Courtney Granner, Illustrator

Award of Excellence
The Washington Post Magazine
Washington, DC
Kelly Doe, Art Director & Designer

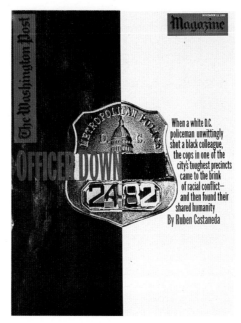

Award of Excellence
The Washington Post Magazine
Washington, DC
Kelly Doe, Art Director & Designer; Karen Tanaka, Photo
Editor; William Duke, Photographer

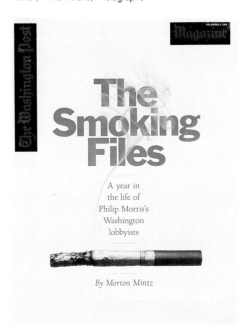

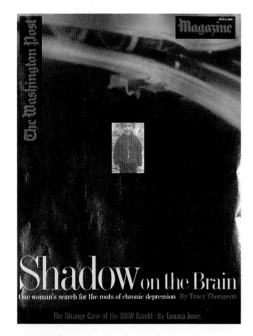

Award of Excellence
The Washington Post Magazine
Washington, DC
Kelly Doe, Art Director & Designer; Ann Elliott Cutting,
Photographer

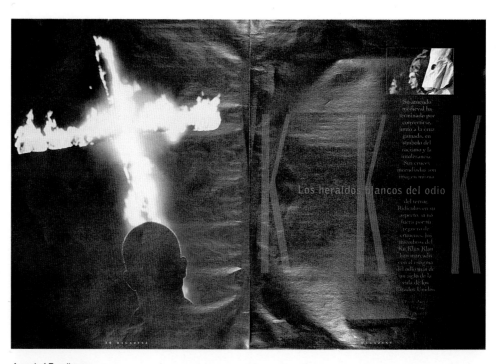

Award of Excellence
El Mundo Magazine
Madrid, Spain
Rodrigo Sánchez, Art Director & Designer; Miguel Buckenmeyer, Designer; Amparo Redondo, Designer

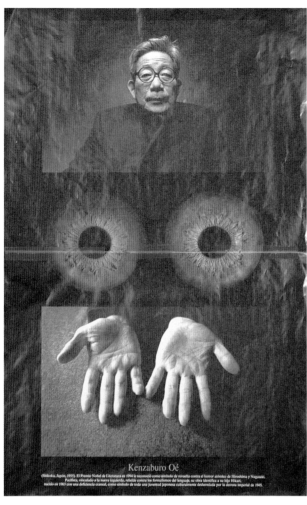

Kenzaburo Oé

(Shikoku, Japón, 1935). El Premio Nobel de Literatura en 1994 le reconoció como símbolo de revuelta contra el horror atómico de Hiroshima y Nagasaki. Pacifista, vinculado a la nueva izquierda, rebelde contra los formalismos del lenguaje, su obra identifica a su hijo Hikari, nacido en 1963 con una deficiencia craneal, como símbolo de toda una juventud japonesa culturalmente deshentada por la derrota imperial de 1945.

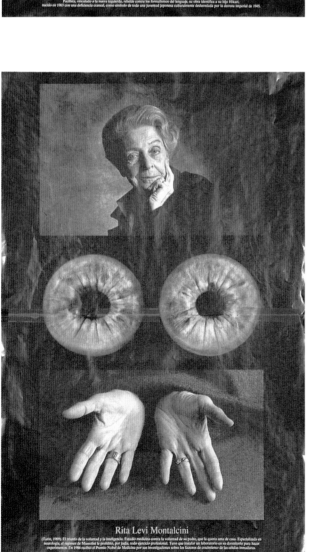

Rita Levi Montalcini

(Turín, 1909). El triunfo de la voluntad y la inteligencia. Estudió medicina contra la voluntad de su padre, que la quería ama de casa. Especializada en neurología, el régimen de Mussolini le prohibió, por judía, todo ejercicio profesional. Tuvo que instalar un laboratorio en su dormitorio para hacer experimentos. En 1986 recibió el Premio Nobel de Medicina por sus investigaciones sobre los factores de crecimiento de las células inmaduras.

Gold

El Pais Semanal

Madrid, Spain

David García, Deputy Editor; Eugenio González, Design Director; Isabel Benito, Designer; Gustavo Sanchez, Designer; Mariapaz Domingo, Designer; José M. Navia, Photo Editor; Francis Giacobetti, Photographer

Camilo José Cela

(Iria Flavia, La Coruña, España, 1916). Goya hecho palabra. Su inmenso talento y su éxito —culminado con el Premio Nobel de Literatura en 1989—, ayudados por su físico y su personalidad, le han convertido en una institución. Tras su aspecto de monumento a sí mismo se esconde un escritor conciorazudo y honesto, profundamente innovador, con una capacidad de trazar caricaturas sociales sólo comparable a la de Valle-Inclán.

Silver

El Mundo Magazine

Madrid, Spain

Rodrigo Sánchez, Art Director & Designer; Miguel Buckenmeyer, Designer; Amparo Redondo, Designer

Silver
• Also Silver for Illustration
**The New York Times
Magazine**
New York, NY
Janet Froelich, Art Director; Joel
Cuyler, Designer; Konstantin
Kakanias, Illustrator

Award of Excellence
El Periodico de Catalunya/El Dominical
Barcelona, Spain
Ferran Sendra, Designer; Ricardo Feriche, Creative Director; Núria Miquel, Designer; Kim Salomon, Designer; Alejandro Yofre, Photo Editor; Héctor Chimirri, News Editor; Rafael Nadal, Vice-Editor; Jorge Represa, Photographer

Es el 'bluesman' vivo más influyente del mundo. Ha llegado a viejo sorteando los abismos. A sus 75 años, se aferra a la vida con escepticismo y a la música con pasión. Sabe mucho Hooker: *"Lo mejor de ser viejo es que se pierde la vergüenza"*, afirma en su casa de Los Ángeles. Su último desafío se llama 'Chill out!' (¡Tranquilo!), un disco que concita las esencias adquiridas en 45 años en la carretera, 100 elepés, 5.000 conciertos, decenas de guitarras, cientos de mujeres, infinitos desengaños e incontables borracheras. ¡Larga vida al viejo John!

Texto: IGNACIO PARA Fotos: JORGE REPRESA

John Lee Hooker

Award of Excellence
The Philadelphia Inquirer Magazine
Philadelphia, PA
Bert Fox, Art Director/Photo Editor; Christine Dunleavy, Design Director/Designer; James Balog, Photographer; Chris Rainer, Photographer

Award of Excellence
The New York Times Magazine
New York, NY
Janet Froelich, Art Director; Lisa Naftolin, Designer; Matthew Rolston, Photographer; Elizabeth Stewart, Stylist

Smoke and Mirrors

Single-subject series winners were based on submissions from three or more consecutive publication dates of pre-planned coverage. Special sections could include news, sports, business and all "soft news" or features special projects. Inside pages were divided into two groups: those with ads or those with no ads.

Special Sections

- Single-Subject Series
- Cover Page
- Inside Page

Silver

The Seattle Times

Seattle, WA

Rick Lund, Design,
Editing; David Miller,
Art Director/Design;
Michael Kellams,
Graphics, Design;
Chris Soprych,
Graphics; Fred Nelson,
Photo Editor; Cole
Porter, Photo Editor;
Cathy Henkel, Editing;
Paul Palazzo, Editing;
Photo Staff

Take it to the limit

In homely Dome, something that's too good to end

Edgar's 2 homers, 7 RBI drive M's into series finale

Misfires in fourth dump Huskies

Don't blame Huard for devastating defeat

O.J. not guilty

M's win West

Fans go wild as Mariners head for playoffs in N.Y.

Machinists reject Boeing's final offer

Award of Excellence

• Also Awards of Excellence for Informational Graphics & Graphics Portfolio

Reforma

México City, Mexico

Juan Jesús Cortés, Illustrator; Ignacio Guerrero, Designer; Daniel Esqueda Guadalajara, Section Designer; Emilio Deheza, Art Director; Eduardo Danilo, Design Consultant; Arturo Jiménez, Graphics Editor; Imágen Latina, Photographer; Homero Fernández, Editor; Ismael García, Editor

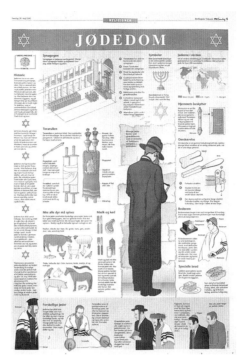

Award of Excellence
San Francisco Examiner
San Francisco, CA
Kelly Frankeny, AME Design; Mark Costantini,
Photographer; Fran Ortiz, Photographer, Don Asmussen,
Artist; Jane Kay, Researcher; Richard Paoli, Photo
Director; Steve Cook, AME Enterprise; Joe Shoulak, Artist;
Art Staff

Award of Excellence
The Virginian-Pilot
Norfolk, VA
Sam Hundley, Designer; Peter Dishal, Designer; Eric
Seidman, Art Director; Pat Dooley, Editor

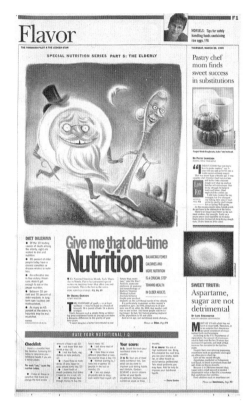

Award of Excellence
The Spokesman-Review
Spokane, WA
John K. Nelson, Design Editor; John Sale, Photo Editor

Silver

The St. Petersburg Times

St. Petersburg, FL

Todd Windsor, Designer; Neville Green, ME/Tampa; Victor Junco, Photographer; Sonya Doctorian, Director of Photography

Award of Excellence

Detroit Free Press

Detroit, MI

Steve Anderson, Sports Design Director; Gene Myers, Sports Editor; Owen Davis, Deputy Sports Editor; Reid Creager, Writer & Copy Editor; Tim Marcinkoski, Copy Editor; John Lowe, Writer; Joe Cybulski, Agate Editor; Jim Dwight, Agate Editor

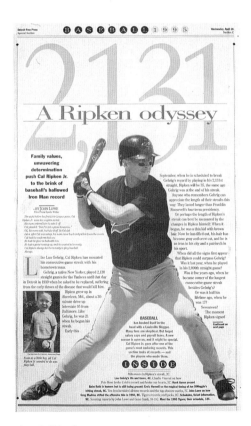

Award of Excellence

The Detroit News

Detroit, MI

David Kordalski, Project Editor; Dale Peskin, Deputy Managing Editor; Chris Willis, Assistant Graphics Editor & Designer; Jamee Tanner, Graphic Journalist; Karen Van Antwerp, Researcher

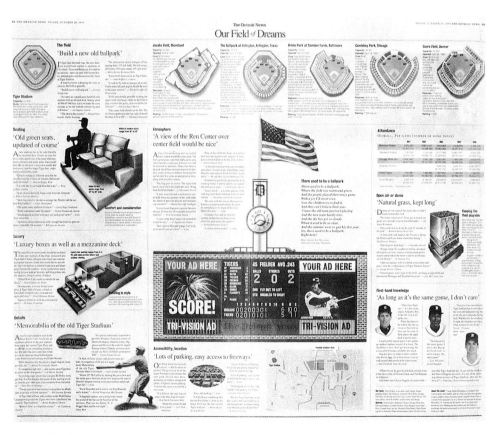

Silver
Democrat and Chronicle
Rochester, NY
Dennis R. Floss, Designer & Special Section Editor; John Gibson, AME Sports; Kevin Smith, Artist; Annette Ney Meade, Researcher; Jim Bliss, Illustrator; Phil Bliss, Illustrator

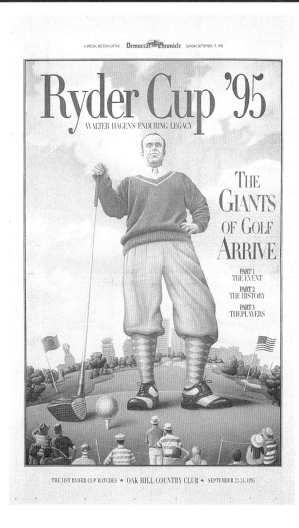

Award of Excellence
● Also Award of Excellence for Reprint
Seattle Post-Intelligencer
Seattle, WA
Duane Hoffman, Art Director; Ben Garrison, Artist/Designer; Kim Carney, Artist/Designer; Steve Greenberg, Artist/Designer; Dave Horsey, Artist/Designer; Dave Gray, Artist/Designe

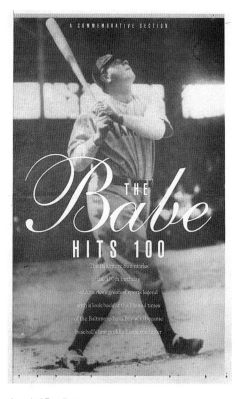

Award of Excellence
The Baltimore Sun
Baltimore, MD
Joseph Hutchinson, AME Graphics/Design; Steve Marcus, Design Editor, Sports

Award of Excellence
The News-Sentinel
Fort Wayne, IN
Sheri Conover Sharlow, Copy Editor; Ellie Bogue, Designer; Ezra Wolfe, Designer; Cindy Jones-Hulfachor, Graphic Reporter; Leisa Thompson, Photographer

Award of Excellence
Dayton Daily News
Dayton, OH
Lee Waigand, Art Director & Designer; Ken Palen, Designer; John Hancock, Gregg Degroat, MB Hopkins, Graphics; Bill Garlow, Photo Ed.; John Thomson, AME Graphics

Award of Excellence
• Also Award of Excellence for Illustration
The Wall Street Journal Reports
New York, NY
Gregory B. Leeds, Design Director; Nikolai Klein, Art Director & Designer; Richard Downs, Illustrator

Award of Excellence
The Toronto Star
Toronto, Canada
Catherine Pike, Designer; Dick Loek, Photographer; Chris Zelkovich, Section Ed.; Dave Ellis, City Ed.; Alan Marshall, Deputy City Ed.; Warren Gerard, Writer; Ian Somerville, Art Director; Catherine Farley, Bob Westover, Map Artists

Award of Excellence
The Augusta Chronicle
Augusta, GA
John Fish, ME; Rick McKee, Graphics Editor; Joseph Trotz, Photo Editor

Award of Excellence
The Baltimore Sun
Baltimore, MD
Joseph Hutchinson, AME Graphics/Design

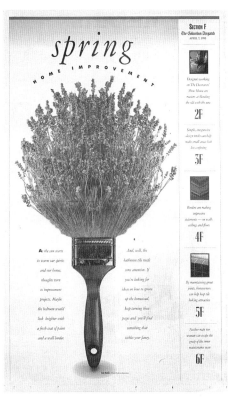

Award of Excellence
• Also Award of Excellence for Combination Portfolio
The Columbus Dispatch
Columbus, OH
Scott Minister, Art Director & Designer; Tom Mattix, Photo Illustration; Becky Kover, Section Coordinator

Silver
• Also Award of Excellence for Special Section/Without Ads
The Dallas Morning News
Dallas, TX
Ben McConnell, Deputy Art Director; Clif Bosler, Graphics & Design; Kathleen Vincent, Art Director; Chris Morris, Graphics & Design; Tom Siegfried, Editor; Karen Patterson, Assistant Editor

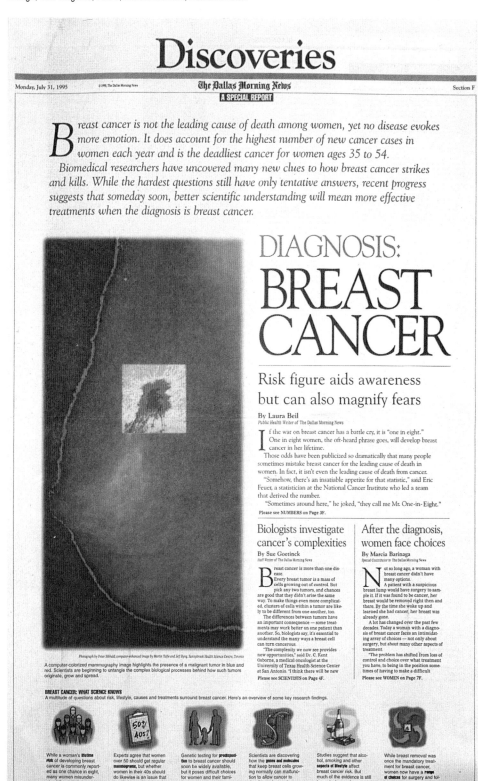

Award of Excellence
The Columbus Dispatch
Columbus, OH
Scott Minister, Art Director; Tricia Barry, Designer

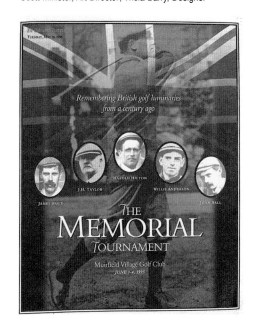

Award of Excellence
The Columbus Dispatch
Columbus, OH
Rod Harris, Designer

Award of Excellence
The Herald-Sun
Durham, NC
Dwayne Purper, Designer

Award of Excellence
The Herald-Sun
Durham, NC
Dwayne Purper, Designer

Award of Excellence
de Volkskrant
Amsterdam, Netherlands
Waldemar Post, Art Director; Ronald Visser, Designer;
Anthony Suau, Photographer

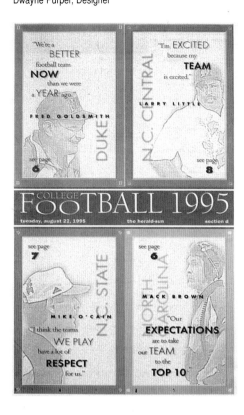

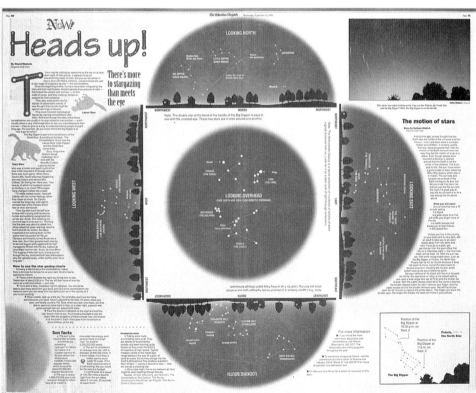

Award of Excellence
The Columbus Dispatch
Columbus, OH
Scott Minister, Art Director; Sherri Saunders, Infographics Designer

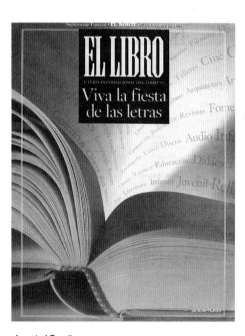

Award of Excellence
El Norte
Monterrey, Mexico
Carmen A. Escobedo, Designer; Juan José Cerón,
Photographer; Arturo López, Photographer; Dolores
Carrillo, Photo-Artist; Raúl Braulio Martinez, Art Director;
Carmen A. Escobedo, Graphics Editor

Award of Excellence
Providence Journal-Bulletin
Providence, RI
Todd Lindeman, Illustrator; Mick Cochran, Art
Direction/Designer

Award of Excellence
The Record
Hackensack, NJ
Ches Wajda, Designer

Award of Excellence
• Also Silver for Illustration
San Jose Mercury News
San Jose, CA
Kris Strawser, Designer & Illustrator

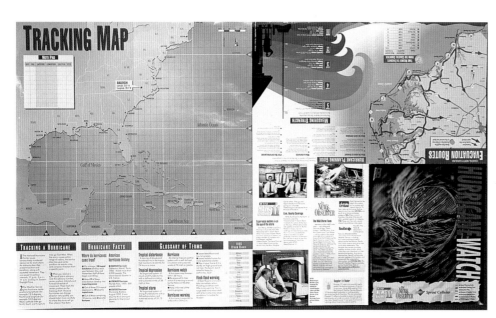

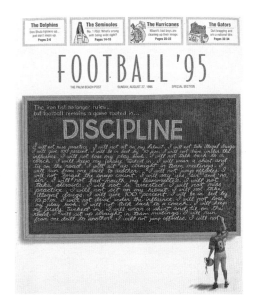

Award of Excellence
The News & Observer
Raleigh, NC
Nam Nguyen, Illustrator & Designer; Ben Estes, Editor; David Pickel, Presentation/Design Editor; Ken Mowry, Graphics
Director

Award of Excellence
The Palm Beach Post
West Palm Beach, FL
Jodi A. Davis, Designer; Sherman Zent, Photographer;
Pete Cross, Photo Director; Dave Barak, Photo Technician;
Tim Burke, Executive Sports Editor; Nick Moschella,
Deputy Sports Editor; Pat Crowley, Cartoonist

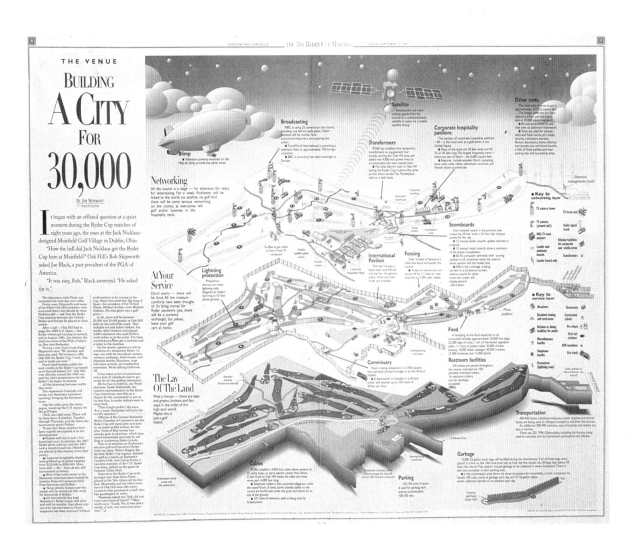

Silver

Democrat and Chronicle
Rochester, NY
Kevin M. Smith, Artist;
Annette Ney Meade,
Researcher; Dennis R. Floss,
Special Projects Editor

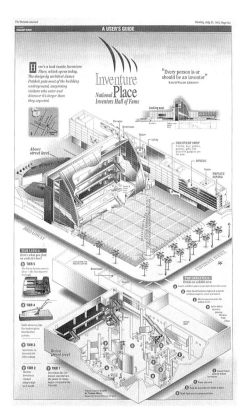

Award of Excellence
Akron Beacon Journal
Akron, OH
Susan Mango Curtis, AME Graphics; Terence Oliver,
Illustrator

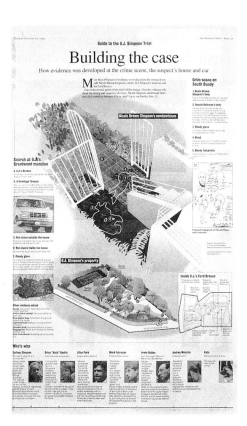

Award of Excellence
• Also Award of Excellence for Informational Graphics
The Detroit News
Detroit, MI
Chris Willis, Asst. Graphics Ed.; Robert Graham, Graphics
Artist; Dale Peskin, DME; Chris Kozlowski, Graphics Ed.;
Shayne Bowman, Asst. Graphics Ed.

Award of Excellence
The Wall Street Journal Reports
New York, NY
Gregory B. Leeds, Design Director; Christopher Bing,
Illustrator

Award of Excellence
Expansion
Madrid, Spain
José Juan Gámez, Design Director; Pablo Ma Ramírez, Designer & Artist; Mar Domingo, Artist; Antonio Martín Hervás, Artist & Designer

Award of Excellence
Los Angeles Times
Los Angeles, CA
Ken Oelerich, Artist; David Montesino, Researcher; Vicky McCargar, Graphics Editor

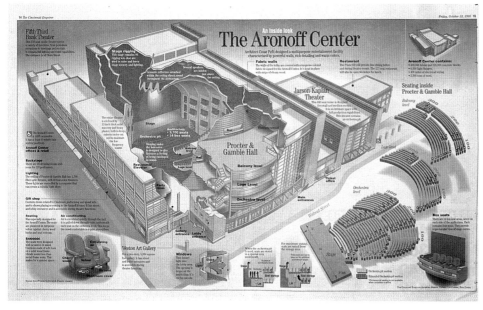

Award of Excellence
The Cincinnati Enquirer
Cincinnati, OH
Jonathan Massie, Art Director; Ron Cosby, Artist; Colleen Lanchester, Designer

Award of Excellence
The Wall Street Journal Reports
New York, NY
Gregory B. Leeds, Design Director; Nikolai Klein, Designer; Ray Bartkus, Illustrator

Award of Excellence
Marca
Madrid, Spain
José Juan Gámez, Design Director; Mar Domingo, Graphic Artist; Miguel A. Fernández,
Graphic Artist

Award of Excellence
Marca
Madrid, Spain
José Juan Gámez, Design Director; Mar Domingo, Artist; Sofia Valgañon, Artist; Miguel
Angel Fernández, Artist; Martina Gil, Artist

Award of Excellence
The Philadelphia Inquirer
Philadelphia, PA
Dave Milne, AME Graphics

Award of Excellence
• Also Award of Excellence for Informational Graphics
Marca
Madrid, Spain
José Juan Gámez, Design Director; César Galera, Graphic Artist

Award of Excellence
The Wall Street Journal Reports
New York, NY
Gregory B. Leeds, Design Director; Nikolai Klein, Art
Director & Designer

Award of Excellence
Wichita Falls Times Record News
Wichita Falls, TX
Scott Johnson, Graphics Editor

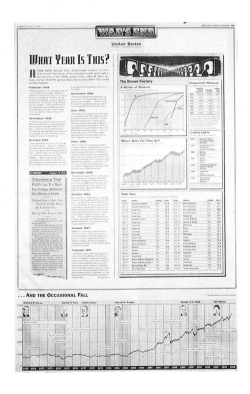

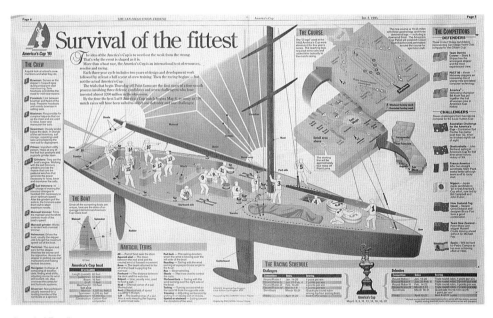

Award of Excellence
• Also Award of Excellence for Informational Graphics Portfolio
The San Diego Union-Tribune
San Diego, CA
Paul Horn, Graphics Journalist

Portfolios had to include six pages by one designer in any one of four areas: News, feature, magazine or a combination of any of these. Entries were divided into three circulation groups: Circulation 175,000 and above, circulation 50,000 through 174,999 and circulation 49,999 and below.

Design Portfolio

- News
- Feature
- Magazine
- Combination

Award of Excellence
Asbury Park Press
Neptune, NJ

Harris Siegel, ME/Design & Photography; Andrew Prendimano, Art & Photo Director; Janet L. Michaud, Designer

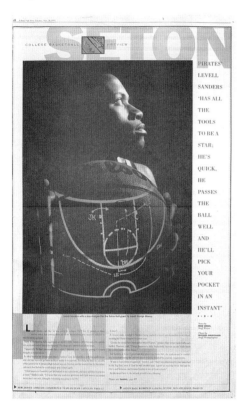

Award of Excellence
The New York Times
New York, NY

Wayne Kamidoi, Designer

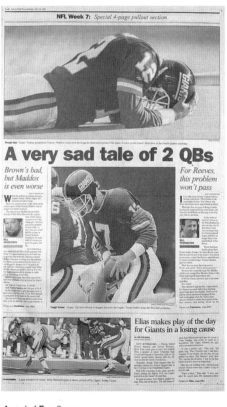

Award of Excellence
Asbury Park Press
Neptune, NJ

Harris Siegel, ME/Design & Photography, Designer;
Andrew Prendimano, Art & Photo Director

CHRISTIAN ROCK/E1

The Virginian-Pilot

8 hurt as Norfolk jail annex collapses

WET CEMENT PARTIALLY BURIES SIX WORKERS

Injuries weren't life-threatening

OSHA WILL INVESTIGATE

HOW IT HAPPENED

"All I was doing was hanging on for dear life"

Experience stunned worker Wayne Alexander.

Why Richmond voted to honor Arthur Ashe on Monument Avenue

Familiar partisan themes emerge, and a surprise: Foster's briefcase

Collapse: "There was nowhere to run"

Workers:
All escaped serious injury

Cement pourings must be inspected. Were rules followed?

LE SOLEIL

LE QUOTIDIEN DE LA CAPITALE

QUÉBEC, LE VENDREDI 1ER DÉCEMBRE 1995

De la visite de l'Assomption au 1080, des Braves

La mairesse Boucher prête à aller en prison
En guerre contre le plancher d'emploi de ses cols bleus

EXCLUSIF ENTREVUE AVEC LE MINISTRE DE L'ÉDUCATION

Un examen d'entrée pour les professeurs

Garon veut vérifier leurs qualifications

Emmanuel volait ses voisins pour bouffer

La grève se durcit en France

Commission de la capitale

ARTS SPECTACLES
LA NOUVELLE
MARIE CARMEN B 1

PARTIR
CHAUDES HUMEURS
DE MARRAKECH D 1

LE SOLEIL

LE QUOTIDIEN DE LA CAPITALE

QUÉBEC, LE SAMEDI 28 OCTOBRE 1995

À l'ombre de la Sun Life

«Q»

RASSEMBLEMENT PANCANADIEN À MONTRÉAL

Ultime appel aux Québécois

Chrétien promet des changements «à l'aube du XXIe siècle»

Entente entre les enseignants de cégep de la CSN et le gouvernement

---

ABORTION RULING
Judge blocks waiting period for new law

THE HAMMOND TIMES

FOOD
New feature lets you 'see' the recipe

TOXIC SCARE IN SCHERERVILLE

■ Residents, workers moved after hazardous chemical spill.
■ Tanker truck that leaked may have been abandoned years ago.
■ Workers may not be able to return to businesses today.

Hundreds evacuated

Residents surprised tanker was allowed to sit so long

One French plane downed as NATO continues pummeling Bosnia Serbs

---

HOBART BABY
Police asking public's help identifying body

THE MERRILLVILLE TIMES

NBA
Robinson says he should be rookie of year

'You tell me, how can anyone have so little respect for human life?'
Terry Jones, medical technician

Why the children?

Nation's rage rises with bomb's death toll

Terror In the Heartland

Explosion update

■ Clinton vows to find the 'evil cowards' responsible.

■ Rescue workers struggle in face of horror. A-4

■ Families wait, hope for word on missing relatives. A-4

■ How to help. A-4

Independence Hill Conservancy District discusses ways to ease costly assessment

Award of Excellence
The Santa Fe New Mexican
Santa Fe, NM
Dagny Scott, News Editor/Designer

Award of Excellence
The News-Sentinel
Fort Wayne, IN
Ezra Wolfe, Designer

Award of Excellence
The Sun
Bremerton, WA
Denise Clifton, Assistant Presentation Editor

8

A Lit Kit

PACK A
GOOD READ
WITH YOUR
SUMMER GEAR

YOUR GUIDE TO LEISURE

June 16, 1995

5 STEPPING UP
AT THE COOK

8 LEAFING THROUGH
SUMMER BOOKS

23 DOING SOLSTICE
ALL OVER TOWN

25 CHECKING OUT
LOCAL MUSIC

Anchorage Daily News

Gold
Anchorage Daily News
Anchorage, AK
Kevin Ellis, Designer; Galie Jean-Louis, Features Design Director

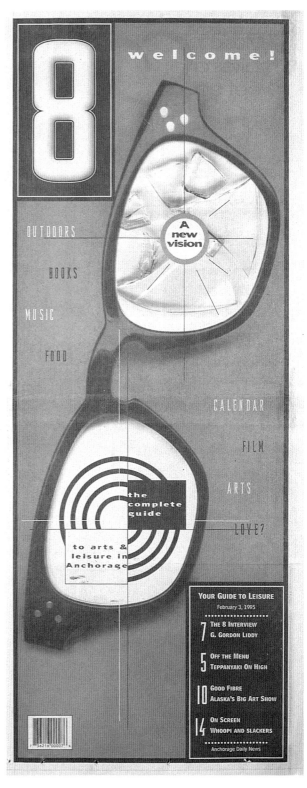

8

welcome!

OUTDOORS

BOOKS

MUSIC

FOOD

A new vision

CALENDAR

FILM

ARTS

LOVE?

the complete guide

to arts & leisure in Anchorage

YOUR GUIDE TO LEISURE

February 3, 1995

7 THE 8 INTERVIEW
G. GORDON LIDDY

5 OFF THE MENU
TEPPANYAKI ON HIGH

10 GOOD FIBRE
ALASKA'S BIG ART SHOW

14 ON SCREEN
WHOOPI AND SLACKERS

Anchorage Daily News

Silver
Le Devoir
Montreal, Canada
Roland-Yves Carignan, Art Director & Designer, Deputy Editor

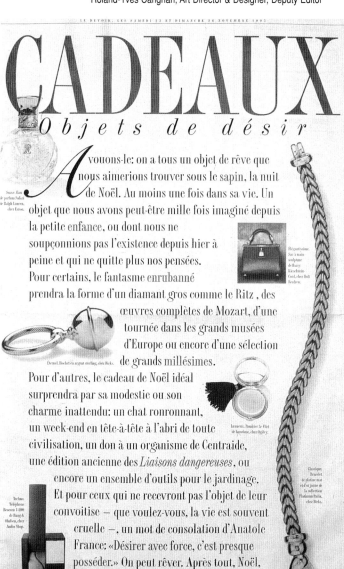

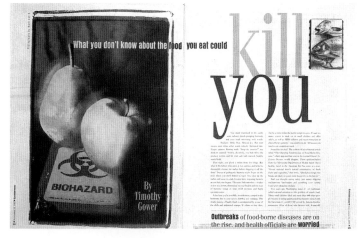

Award of Excellence
Eastsideweek
Seattle, WA
Barbara Dow, Art Director & Designer; Mark Widmer, Illustrator

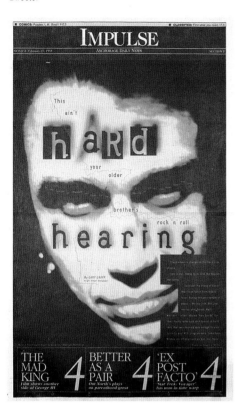

Award of Excellence
The Budapest Sun
Budapest, Hungary
Craig Snelgrove, Designer

Award of Excellence
El Mensajero
San Francisco, CA
Douglas Beach, Art Director

Award of Excellence
El Mundo
Madrid, Spain
Carmelo Caderot, Art Director/Design

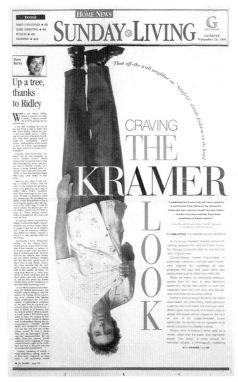

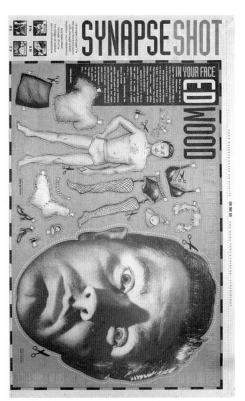

Award of Excellence
Le Devoir
Montreal, Canada
Roland-Yves Carignan, Page Designer; Jean-Pierre Legault, DME/Art Director

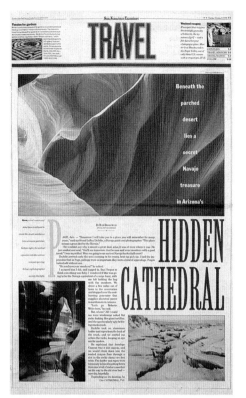

Award of Excellence
San Francisco Examiner
San Francisco, CA
Kelly Frankeny, AME Design; Don McCartney, Designer

Award of Excellence
The Star-Ledger
Newark, NJ
Bob Bogert, Designer

Award of Excellence
• Also Silver for Illustration
The Wall Street Journal Reports
New York, NY
Gregory B. Leeds, Design Director; Dolores Fairman,
Illustrator

Award of Excellence
• Also Award of Excellence for Feature Page
SF Weekly
San Francisco, CA
Kim Klein, Art Director; Pamela Gentile, Photographer

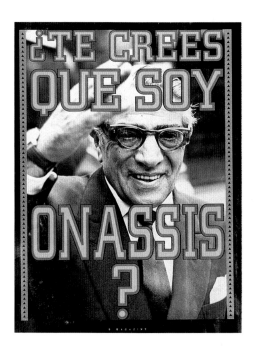

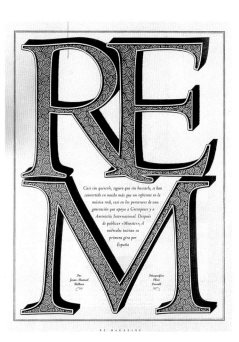

Award of Excellence
El Mundo
Madrid, Spain
Miguel Buckenmeyer, Designer

Silver
• Also Award of Excellence for Magazine Pages
El Mundo
Madrid, Spain
Rodrigo Sanchez, Art Director &
Designer; Miguel Buckenmeyer,
Designer; Amparo Redondo, Designer

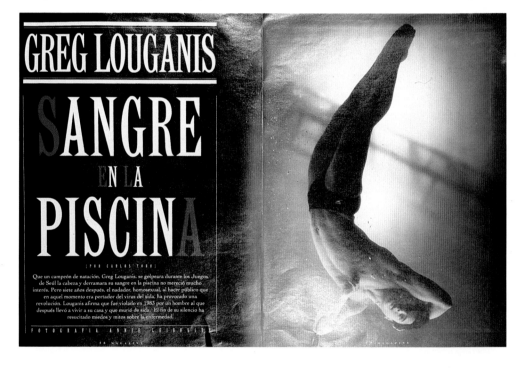

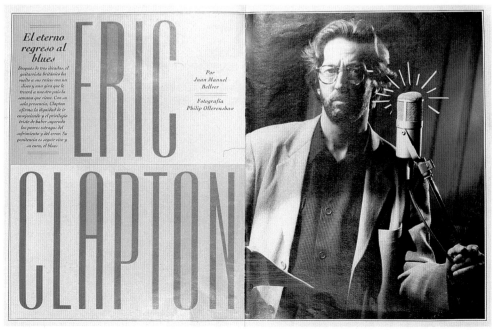

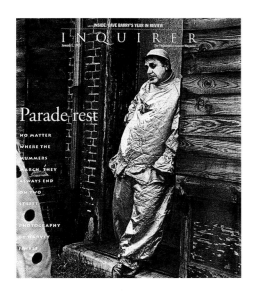

Award of Excellence
The Philadelphia Inquirer Magazine
Philadelphia, PA
Bert Fox, Art Director & Designer

Award of Excellence
The Philadelphia Inquirer Magazine
Philadelphia, PA
Christine Dunleavy, Design Director & Designer

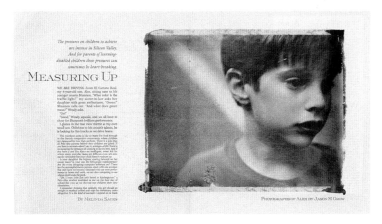

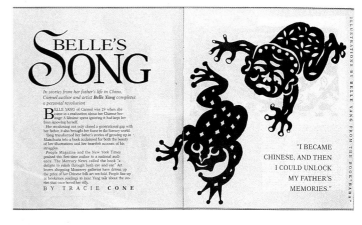

Award of Excellence
San Jose Mercury News
San Jose, CA
Tracy Cox, Art Director & Designer; Sue Morrow, Photo Editor; Jason M. Grow, Photographer; Jim Genshimer, Photographer; Joe Saxe, Illustrator; Belle Yang, Illustrator

Award of Excellence
The Baltimore Sun
Baltimore, MD
Joseph Hutchinson, AME Graphics/Design

Award of Excellence
The Orange County Register
Santa Ana, CA
David Medzerian, Design Team Leader

Award of Excellence
The Cincinnati Enquirer
Cincinnati, OH
Colleen Lanchester, Designer

Work must have been staff-generated or first-use. Entries were divided into two groups: Black and white and/or one color, two or more colors. six pieces of work must have been submitted for each portfolio. Portfolio entries were divided into two groups: Portfolio by one artist, portfolio by more than one artist.

Illustration

- Black & White and/or One Color
- Two or More Colors
- Portfolio by One Artist
- Portfolio by More Than One Artist

Silver
The Globe and Mail
Toronto, Canada
Victor Gad, Illustrator; Eric Nelson, Art Director & Designer; Sarah Murdoch, Focus Editor

Silver
El Mundo
Madrid, Spain
Raul Arias, Illustrator

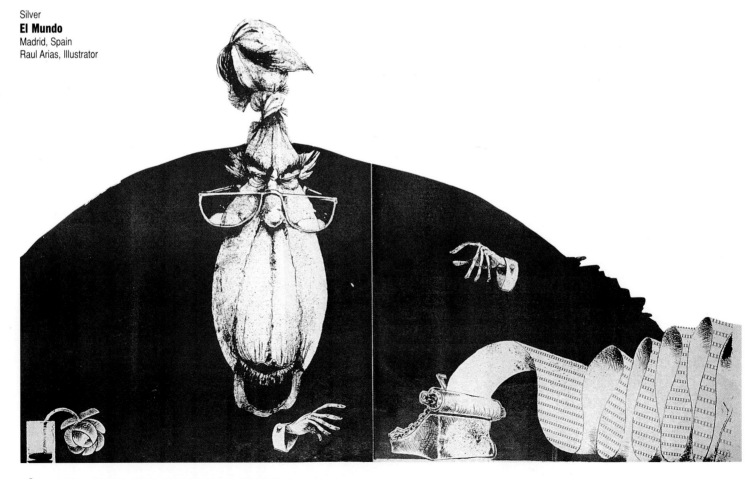

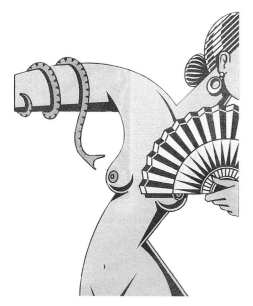

Award of Excellence
El Mundo
Madrid, Spain
Ricardo Martinez, Illustration Director

Award of Excellence
El Mundo
Madrid, Spain
Gorka Sampedro, Illustrator; Carmelo Caderot, Art Director
& Designer; Manuel de Miguel, Designer

Award of Excellence
El Mundo
Madrid, Spain
Ricardo Martinez, Illustration Director

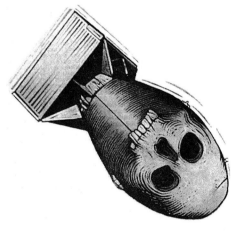

Award of Excellence
The Miami Herald
Miami, FL
Patterson Clark, Artist; Rich Bard, Viewpoint Editor; Randy
Stano, Director of Editorial Art & Design

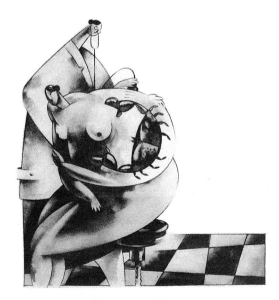

Award of Excellence
El Mundo
Madrid, Spain
Toño Benavides, Illustrator

Award of Excellence
El Nuevo Día
San Juan, PR
Stanley Coll, Illustrator; José L. Díaz de Villegas,
Sr., Art Director & Designer

Award of Excellence
The Miami Herald
Miami, FL
Patterson Clark, Artist; Rich Bard, Viewpoint Editor; Randy
Stano, Director of Editorial Art & Design

Award of Excellence
The Miami Herald
Miami, FL
Patterson Clark, Artist; Rich Bard, Viewpoint Editor; Randy
Stano, Director of Editorial Art & Design

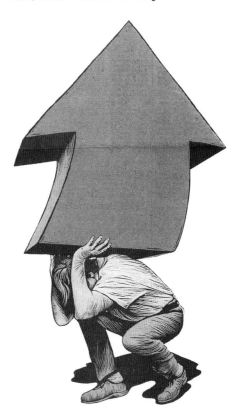

Award of Excellence
Eskilstuna-Kuriren
Eskilstuna, Sweden
Lennart Strand, Senior Editor

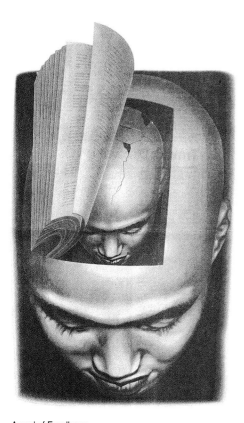

Award of Excellence
The Oregonian
Portland, OR
Steve Cowden, Artist; Shawn Vitt, Art Director

Award of Excellence
Reforma
México City, Mexico
Fabricio Vanden Broeck, Illustrator; Roberto Zamarripa,
Editor; Ricardo del Castillo, Section Designer; Emilio
Deheza, Art Director; Eduardo Danilo, Design Consultant

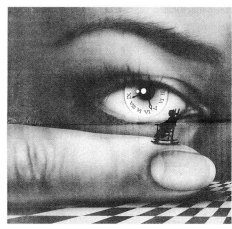

Award of Excellence
El Nuevo Dia
San Juan, PR
Stanley Coll, Illustrator; Jose' L. Diaz de Villegas, Sr., Art
Director & Designer

Award of Excellence
Pittsburgh Post-Gazette
Pittsburgh, PA
Stacy Innerst, Illustrator; Tracy Collins, Associate
Editor/Graphics; Bill Pliske, Deputy Editor/Graphics; Anita
Dufalla, Art Director; Christopher Pett-Ridge, AME
Graphics

Award of Excellence
The Wall Street Journal Reports
New York, NY
Gregory B. Leeds, Design Director; Christopher Bing,
Illustrator

Award of Excellence
Pittsburgh Post-Gazette
Pittsburgh, PA
Stacy Innerst, Illustrator; Tracy Collins, Associate
Editor/Graphics; Bill Pliske, Deputy Editor/Graphics; Anita
Dufalla, Art Director; Christopher Pett-Ridge, AME
Graphics

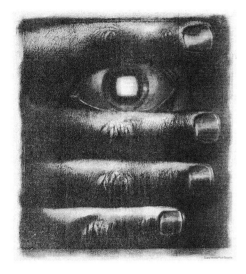

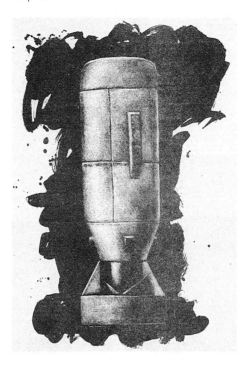

Award of Excellence
Pittsburgh Post-Gazette
Pittsburgh, PA
Daniel Marsula, Illustrator; Tracy Collins, Associate
Editor/Graphics; Bill Pliske, Deputy Editor/Graphics; Anita
Dufalla, Art Director; Christopher Pett-Ridge,
AME/Graphics

Award of Excellence
San Jose Mercury News
San Jose, CA
Tracy Cox, Art Director; Sue Morrow, Designer; Nuri
Ducassi, Illustrator

Award of Excellence
Pittsburgh Post-Gazette
Pittsburgh, PA
Stacy Innerst, Illustrator; Tracy Collins, Associate
Editor/Graphics; Bill Pliske, Deputy Editor/Graphics; Anita
Dufalla, Art Director; Christopher Pett-Ridge, AME
Graphics

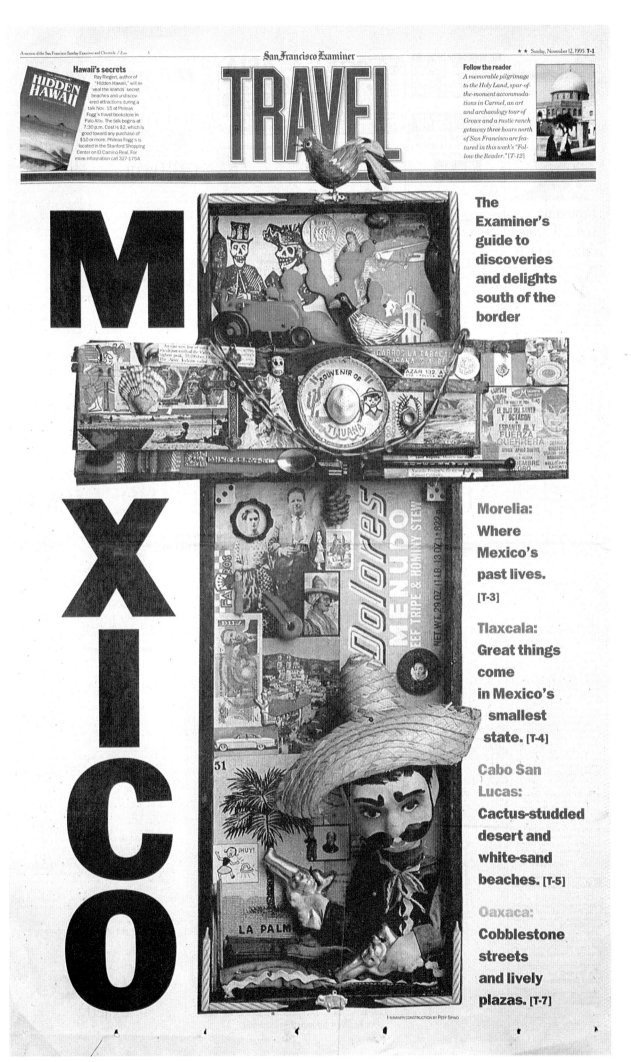

A section of the San Francisco Sunday Examiner and Chronicle / Zone 5

San Francisco Examiner

TRAVEL

★ ★ Sunday, November 12, 1995 **T-1**

Hawaii's secrets

Ray Riegert, author of "Hidden Hawaii," will reveal the islands' secret beaches and undiscovered attractions during a talk Nov. 15 at Phileas Fogg's travel bookstore in Palo Alto. The talk begins at 7:30 p.m. Cost is $2, which is good toward any purchase of $10 or more. Phileas Fogg's is located in the Stanford Shopping Center on El Camino Real. For more information call 327-1754

Follow the reader

A memorable pilgrimage to the Holy Land, spur-of-the-moment accommodations in Carmel, an art and archaeology tour of Greece and a rustic ranch getaway three hours north of San Francisco are featured in this week's "Follow the Reader." [T-12]

MEXICO

The Examiner's guide to discoveries and delights south of the border

Morelia: Where Mexico's past lives. [T-3]

Tlaxcala: Great things come in Mexico's smallest state. [T-4]

Cabo San Lucas: Cactus-studded desert and white-sand beaches. [T-5]

Oaxaca: Cobblestone streets and lively plazas. [T-7]

EXAMINER CONSTRUCTION BY PETE SPINO

Silver
**The New York Times
Magazine**
New York, NY
Janet Froelich, Art Director;
Joel Cuyler, Designer; Philip
Burke, Illustrator

Silver
El Mundo
Madrid, Spain
Gorka Sampedro, Illustrator

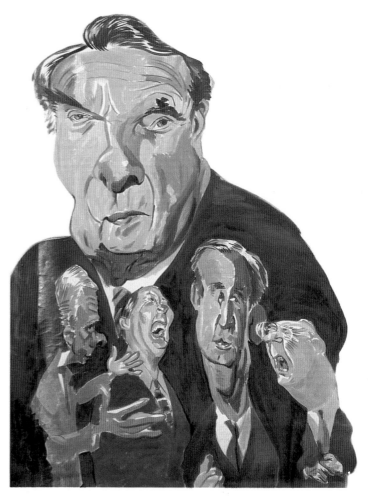

Silver
El Pais Semanal
Madrid, Spain
Eugenio González, Design Director; Isabel Benito, Designer; Gustavo Sánchez, Designer;
Mariapaz Domingo, Designer; Luz Sanchez-Mellado, Editor

Silver
The New York Times Magazine
New York, NY
Benoit , Illustrator; Linda Brewer, Art Director

Silver
San Jose Mercury News
San Jose, CA
Nuri J. Ducassi, Designer, Illustrator & Design Director

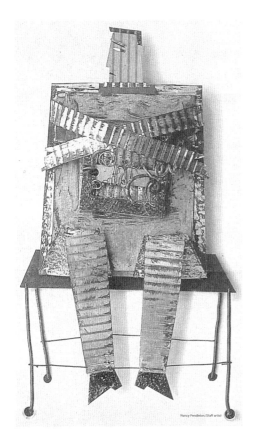

Award of Excellence
Baltimore Jewish Times
Baltimore, MD
Don Arday, Illustrator; Robyn Katz, Art Director

Award of Excellence
The Arizona Republic/The Phoenix Gazette
Phoenix, AZ
Nancy Pendleton, Artist; Don Renfroe, Designer

Award of Excellence
The Chicago Tribune
Chicago, IL
Nancy J. Canfield, Creative Director; Steven Brodner, Illustrator; Denis Gosselin, Editor; Douglas Balz, ME; Brenda Butler, Senior Features Editor; Kirt Weed, Art Director; Margaret Carroll, Assistant Editor; Clarence Petersen, Assistant Editor; Anna Seeto, Production Asst.

Award of Excellence
El Mundo
Madrid, Spain
Victoria Martos, Illustrator

Award of Excellence
Chicago Tribune
Chicago, IL
Sam Hundley, Illustrator; Joan Cairney, Art Director

Award of Excellence
El Mundo
Madrid, Spain
Toño Benavides, Illustrator

Award of Excellence
El Mundo
Madrid, Spain
Victoria Martos, Illustrator

Award of Excellence
The Globe and Mail/Report on Business Magazine
Toronto, Canada
Kaspar deLine, Art Director; Gary Clement, Illustrator; David Olive, Editor; Trevor Cole, Writer

Award of Excellence
The Hartford Courant
Hartford, CT
James Steinberg, Illustrator; Christian Potter Drury, Art
Director

Award of Excellence
The New York Times Magazine
New York, NY
Janet Froelich, Art Director; Nancy Harris, Designer; Julian
Allen, Illustrator

Award of Excellence
The New York Times
New York, NY
Tim Bower, Illustrator; Steven Heller, Art Director

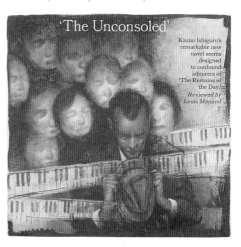

Award of Excellence
San Jose Mercury News
San Jose, CA
Tracy Cox, Art Director, Designer & Illustrator

Award of Excellence
The Globe and Mail/Report on Business Magazine
Toronto, Canada
Kaspar deLine, Art Director; Amanda Duffy, Illustrator; David Olive, Editor; Domenic Macri, Designer;
Paul Krugman, Writer

Award of Excellence
The News & Observer
Raleigh, NC
Nam Nguyen, Illustrator; Ken Mowry, Graphics Director;
David Pickel, Presentation/Design Editor

Award of Excellence
San Francisco Examiner
San Francisco, CA
Kelly Frankeny, AME Design; Pete Spino, Illustrator &
Designer; Jo Mancuso, Habitat Editor

Award of Excellence
NRC Handelsblad - Zaterdags Bijvoegsel
Rotterdam, Netherlands
Karin Mathijsen Gerst, Design Editor; Ron van Roon,
Illustrator

Award of Excellence
Sun-Sentinel/Sunshine Magazine
Ft. Lauderdale, FL
Ted Pitts, Illustrator; Greg Carannante, Art Director

Award of Excellence
San Jose Mercury News
San Jose, CA
Tracy Cox, Art Director; Sue Morrow, Designer; Nuri
Ducassi, Illustrator

Award of Excellence
Sun-Sentinel/Sunshine Magazine
Ft. Lauderdale, FL
Ted Pitts, Illustrator; Greg Carannante, Art Director

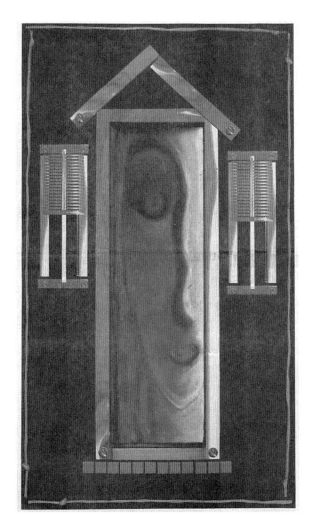

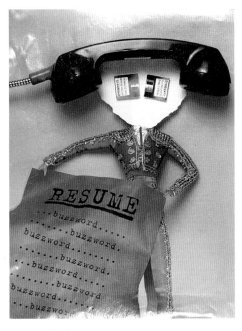

Silver
The Albuquerque Tribune
Albuquerque, NM
Jeff Neumann,
Illustrator

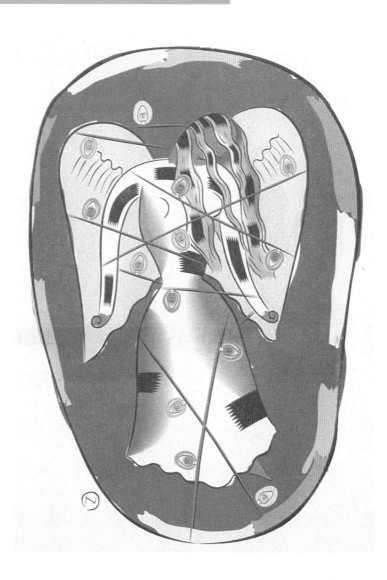

Silver
El Mundo
Madrid, Spain
Ana Juan, Illustrator

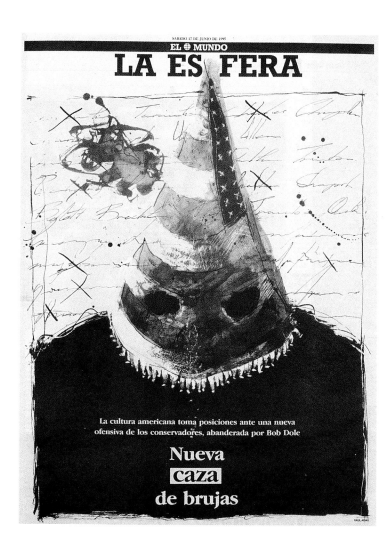

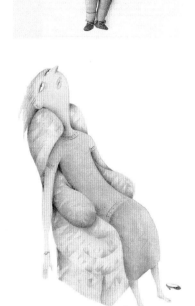

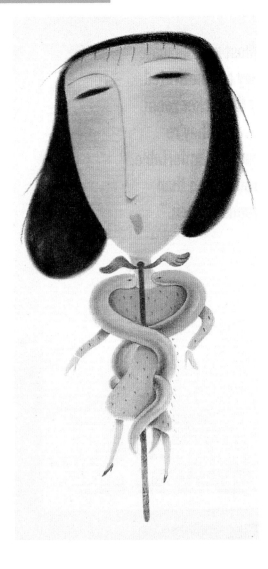

Silver
San Jose Mercury News
San Jose, CA
Sydney Fischer, Illustrator; Tracy Cox, Art Director & Designer

Silver
The Virginian-Pilot
Norfolk, VA
Sam Hundley, Illustrator; Denis
Finley, Copy Editor; Joan
Cairney, Designer; Gail Griffin,
Designer; Marvin Lake, Editor

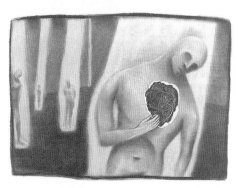

Award of Excellence
• Also Award of Excellence for Illustration
Anchorage Daily News
Anchorage, AK
Dee Boyles, Illustrator & Designer; Galie Jean-Louis,
Features Design Director

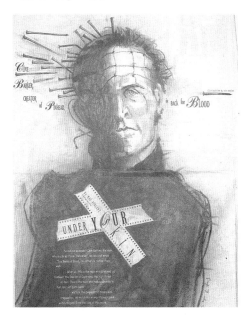

Perspective

Arkansas Democrat 🖉 Gazette

A BIG BANK GOES BUST
Shattered!

How reckless trading
by a junior employee
bankrupted Britain's
oldest investment bank
and left the financial
community digging
through the rubble
for answers.

BY RICHARD W. STEVENSON
New York Times News Service

PHOTO ILLUSTRATION
BY KIRK MONTGOMERY
Arkansas Democrat-Gazette

Perspective

Arkansas Democrat 🖉 Gazette

Field
of
schemes

Where have you gone, Joe DiMaggio?
And Babe Ruth? In this era
of shifting players and teams,
where the heroes are spoiled fools,
has sports lost its dream and purpose?

BY ROBERT LIPSYTE
The New York Times Magazine

ILLUSTRATION BY KIRK MONTGOMERY
Arkansas Democrat-Gazette

Award of Excellence
• Also Award of Excellence for Opinion Page
Arkansas Democrat-Gazette
Little Rock, AR
Kirk Montgomery, AME Art/Design; Van W. Holcombe,
Chief Page Designer/Features

Award of Excellence
El Mundo
Madrid, Spain
Toño Benavides, Illustrator

Vivir al
límite

Los jóvenes se desmelenan
durante los fines de semana.
Buscan diversión y desafío.
LA GENERACIÓN X

Adictos
al
juego

Award of Excellence
El Mundo
Madrid, Spain
Samuel Velasco, Illustrator

Award of Excellence
El Pais Semanal
Madrid, Spain
Eugenio Gonzalez, Design Director; Isabel Benito, Designer; Gustavo Sanchez, Designer; Mariapaz Domingo, Designer; Angel de Pedro, Illustrator

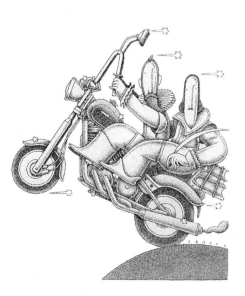

Award of Excellence
• Also Award of Excellence for Illustration
El Mundo
Madrid, Spain
Ulises Culebro, Illustrator

Award of Excellence
El Periódico de Catalunya/El Dominical
Barcelona, Spain
Martin Tognola, Illustrator

Award of Excellence
El Pais
Madrid, Spain
Emma Fernandez, Illustrator

Award of Excellence
El Periodico de Catalunya/El Dominical
Barcelona, Spain
Leonard Beard, Illustrator

Silver
• Also Award of Excellence for Illustration
El Mundo
Madrid, Spain
Toño Benavides, Illustrator; Gorka Sampedro, Illustrator; Ulises Culebro, Illustrator; Samuel Velasco, Illustrator

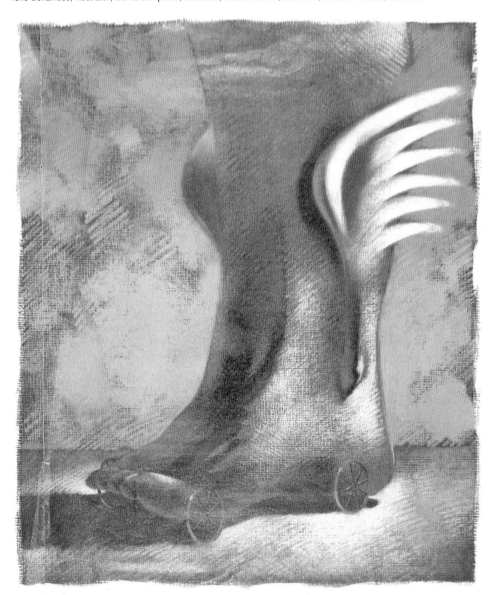

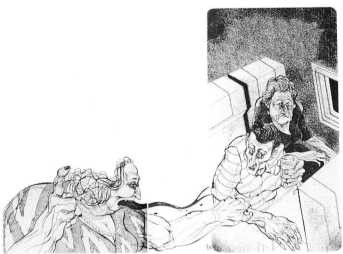

Award of Excellence
El Pais
Madrid, Spain
Gusi Bejer, Illustrator

Silver

Philadelphia Inquirer Magazine

Philadelphia, PA

Gregory Manchess, Illustrator; Christine Dunleavy, Design Director; Brad Holland, Illustrator; Gerard DuBois, Illustrator; Polly Becker, Illustrator; Stasys Eidrigevicus, Illustrator; Courtney Granner, Illustrator

EL CONSTITUCIONAL AFILA SUS UÑAS

PEDRO J. RAMIREZ

Endocrinología / La testosterona podría utilizarse para tratar la menopausia • 7

BIOLOGIA
DE LA AGRESIVIDAD

Tras los genes de la ira

Los científicos investigan hasta dónde el ADN predispone a la violencia

PATRICIA MATEY

Silver

• Also Award of Excellence for Illustration

El Mundo

Madrid, Spain

Gorka Sampedro, Illustrator; Ricardo Martínez, Illustrator

Silver
The New York Times Magazine
New York, NY
Janet Froelich, Art Director; Catherine Gilmore-Barnes, Designer; Thomas Woodruff, Illustrator; Gary Panter, Illustrator; Brenda Zlamany, Illustrator; Marshall Arisman, Illustrator; David Levinthal, Photographer

Award of Excellence
The New York Times
New York, NY
Steven Heller, Art Director; Spitting Image Workshop, Illustrator; Brad Holland, Illustrator; Melissa Meier, Illustrator; Jeffrey Fisher, Illustrator; Ray Bartkus, Illustrator; Robert Grossman

Stuck in the Here and Now

Richard Ford's hero yearns for permanence, but not this kind of permanence.

INDEPENDENCE DAY
By Richard Ford
451 pp. New York:
Alfred A. Knopf. $24.

By Charles Johnson

WHEN we last saw Frank Bascombe, the angst-ridden antihero of Richard Ford's highly praised 1986 novel, "The Sportswriter," he was 38 and about to cast himself adrift. A journalist and onetime short-story writer, Frank was a perfectly ordinary man with an extraordinary gift for social observation. Served up in highly original language, his perception lifted him above what he called "the normal applauseless life" to illuminate the "psychic detachment" caused by his divorce and by his own relentless self-doubt. At the time, "The Sportswriter" was an entertaining CAT scan of the shellshocked American psyche. It remains so today.

And now there's a sequel. Frank has returned, 44 years old but still unconvinced that "life's leading someplace," to narrate Mr. Ford's spirited fifth novel, "Independence Day." The time is 1988, and Frank is looking forward to the Fourth of July weekend, when he's arranged to meet with his girlfriend, Sally Caldwell, and then take his 19-year-old son, Paul, to the basketball and baseball Halls of

Continued on page 28

Charles Johnson's novel "Middle Passage" won the 1990 National Book Award for fiction.

8

Work represented in this category has to be staff-generated or first-use. Portfolio entries must have included six pieces of work in one of two divisions: work by one photographer or work by more than one photographer. Staged or electronically manipulated photography must have been entered in the photo illustration division to be considered.

Photojournalism

- Spot News
- Feature
- Photo Story
- Photo Illustration
- Portfolio

Silver
Dagens Nyheter
Stockholm, Sweden
Erich Stering,
Photographer

Award of Excellence
Austin American-Statesman
Austin, TX
Tom Lankes, Photographer; Zach Ryall, Photo Director; G.W. Babb, Design Director

Award of Excellence
The Bakersfield Californian
Bakersfield, CA
Henry Barrios, Photographer

Man nabbed after leap from falls

GADSDEN TIMES / STEVE LATHAM
Gadsden police officer Kenneth Pollard tackles Marty Wagner, 21, of Fort Payne, knocking him into the pool below Noccalula Falls on Friday. Wagner jumped from the top of the falls and eluded police by swimming in the pool and climbing on rocks for approximately an hour.

Second standoff involving Fort Payne man ends safely.

By Donna Maltbie
Times Staff Writer

Police say a Fort Payne man was seeking attention, not injury to himself, when he jumped from Noccalula Falls Friday and stayed just out of officers' reach for almost an hour.

Marty Wagner, 21, held police at bay for three hours July 2 in what police believed was a serious attempt to jump to his death.

This time, Gadsden Police Lt. Randy Phillips said, he was just after publicity.

Wagner threatened to jump last month, but was grabbed by an officer just when officers believed he was about to go.

This time, he did jump, but on the opposite side of the statue of Princess Noccalula.

Legend has it Noccalula leapt to her death because her father would not let her marry a brave from another tribe.

At the time of Wagner's previous jump attempt, he reportedly told an onlooker he was distraught because his ex-girlfriend was getting married.

Friday, Wagner landed in the water unharmed, leaving his shirt hanging on the fence and his battered athletic shoes and socks on the ledge.

Police were called and responded quickly, as did Gadsden firefighters.

Officers went into the gorge and began talking to Wagner, who perched himself on a steeply angled rock.

He stayed there for some time as a crowd gathered along the fences on both sides of the gorge. He appeared to be playing to the crowd much of the time, singing and swaying, throwing open his arms and calling up, "Anybody want to go swimming? I'll invite you for a nice

FALLS continued on A3

GADSDEN TIMES / STEVE LATHAM
Gadsden police officers Kenneth Pollard and Tommy Hammonds wrestle with Marty Wagner after Pollard knocked him into the pool below Noccalula Falls with a diving tackle.

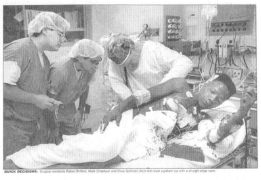

QUICK DECISIONS: Surgical residents Robert Binford, Mark Chastaun and Dave Schindel (from left) treat a patient cut with a straight-edge razor.

Wishard Memorial Hospital's emergency staff comes together to treat severely injured patients.

TEAMING UP on TRAUMA

Photos by Patrick Schneider · Story by Suzanne Reeder

Staring at the placid face lying motionless under the white sheet, the woman whispers a few simple words that serve as a painful farewell.

"That's my brother," she stoically confirms to a nurse and chaplain who have seen more than their share of family members identify loved ones in the trauma center at Wishard Memorial Hospital.

The 31-year-old gunshot victim died minutes after being brought to Wishard, despite the emergency efforts made by paramedics and the hospital staff.

With major injuries, such as gunshot or stab wounds, Wishard's trauma team of surgeons, nurses and specialists race to save a patient. When time and circumstances aren't on their side, the staff has to accept death as an inevitable outcome.

Wishard's ER, the busiest in the state, treats 100,000 patients annually. Their conditions range from life-threatening burns to minor nosebleeds.

For the approximately 2,000 critically

RUSH TO HELP: Wishard paramedics Jane Pogue (left) and Frank Lambert work to stabilize a 29-year-old male with multiple knife wounds.

See TRAUMA Page 4

Award of Excellence
The Press Democrat
Santa Rosa, CA
Chad Surmick, Photographer

Award of Excellence
The Muskegon Chronicle
Muskegon, MI
Dave Carlson, Photographer; Greg Dorsett, Photo Editor

Award of Excellence
The News Tribune
Tacoma, WA
Russ Carmack, Photographer

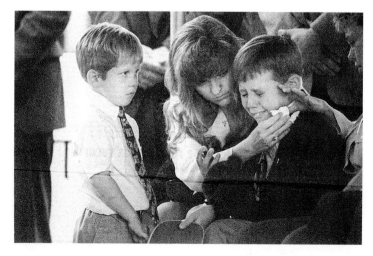

Award of Excellence
The News & Observer
Raleigh, NC
Gary Allen, Photographer; John Hansen, Photo Director; David Pickel, Presentation/Design
Editor

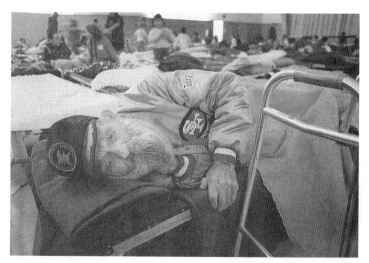

Award of Excellence
The Press Democrat
Santa Rosa, CA
John Burgess, Photographer

Award of Excellence
The San Diego Union-Tribune
San Diego, CA
Eduardo Contreras, Photographer

Award of Excellence
The Orlando Sentinel
Orlando, FL
Gary Bogdon, Senior Photographer; Joan Andrews, Assistant Sports Editor

Award of Excellence
Newsday
Melville, NY
Bill Davis, Photographer

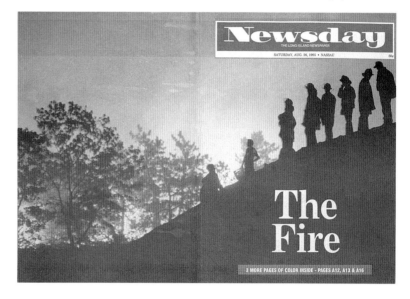

Award of Excellence
The Press Democrat
Santa Rosa, CA
Chad Surmick, Photographer

Award of Excellence
The San Diego Union-Tribune
San Diego, CA
Don Kohlbauer, Photographer

Award of Excellence
The Times-Picayune
New Orleans, LA
John McCusker, Photographer; Doug Parker, Photo Editor;
George Berke, Design Director

Award of Excellence
The Times-Picayune
New Orleans, LA
Eliot Kamenitz, Photographer; Doug Parker, Photo Editor;
Cathy Jenevein, Designer

Award of Excellence
The Times-Picayune
New Orleans, LA
Ellis Lucia, Photographer; Doug Parker, Photo Editor;
James O'Byrne, Sunday News Editor

OPAL PACKS A PUNCH

Storm slams Florida; at least 1 dead

By LESLIE WILLIAMS

N.O. area watches, waits, worries

By COLEMAN WARNER

Award of Excellence
The San Diego Union-Tribune
San Diego, CA
Eduardo Contreras, Photographer

A Sea Cliff home tumbles Monday into the sinkhole caused by the torrent of water seen rushing, top left, from a broken 100-year-old sewer main. The posh neighborhood has been evacuated as more houses teeter on the edge of the expanding chasm. One of the houses in jeopardy has been identified as the boyhood home of photographer Ansel Adams — its owners were awoken by the roar of water as it broke through the pipe.

Award of Excellence
San Francisco Examiner
San Francisco, CA
Richard Paoli, Photo Director; Kelly Frankeny, AME Design; Mark Constantini, Photographer

Silver
**The New York Times
Magazine**
New York, NY
Janet Froelich, Art Director;
Joel Cuyler, Designer; Anthony
Suau, Photographer; Kathy
Ryan, Photo Editor

Award of Excellence
El Pais Semanal
Madrid, Spain
Eugenio Gonzalez, Design Director; Isabel Benito, Designer; Gustavo
Sanchez, Designer; Mariapaz Domingo, Designer; Chema Conesa,
Photographer; Rosa Montero, Editor

Award of Excellence
The New York Times Magazine
New York, NY
Janet Froelich, Art Director; Kathy Ryan, Photo Editor; Karen Kuehn,
Photographer

Award of Excellence
Göteborgs-Posten
Goteborg, Sweden
Lisa Thanner, Photographer;
Gunilla Wernhamn, Designer

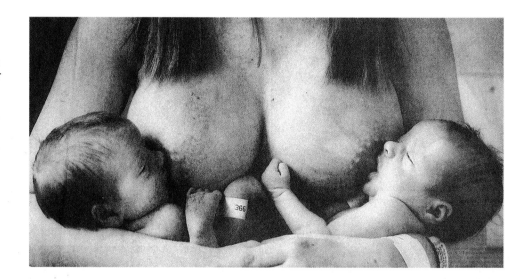

Award of Excellence
The New York Times
New York, NY
Gregory Heisler, Photographer; Linda Brewer, Art Director; Cathy
Mather, Photo Editor

Award of Excellence
El Pais Semanal
Madrid, Spain
Eugenio Gonzalez, Design Director; Isabel Benito, Designer; Gustavo Sanchez, Designer;
David Garcia, Deputy Editor; Mariapaz Domingo, Designer; Jose M. Navia, Picture Editor;
Ricky Davila, Photographer; Manuel Rivas, Editor

The New York Times Magazine
New York, NY
Janet Froelich, Art Director; Leah Lococo, Designer; Josef Astor,
Photographer; Robert Bryan, Stylist

The Philadelphia Inquirer Magazine
Philadelphia, PA
Bert Fox, Art Director/Photo Editor; Christine Dunleavy, Design Director; Michael S. Wirtz,
Photographer; Sue Syrnick, Designer

The New York Times Magazine
New York, NY
Janet Froelich, Art Director; Dominique Issermann,
Photographer; Elizabeth Stewart, Stylist; Joel Cuyler,
Designer

The New York Times Magazine
New York, NY
Janet Froelich, Art Director; Catherine Gilmore-Barnes,
Designer; Sebastião Salgado, Photographer; Kathy Ryan,
Photo Editor

Award of Excellence
The Press Democrat
Santa Rosa, CA
John Burgess, Photographer

Award of Excellence
The San Diego Union-Tribune
San Diego, CA
Sean M. Haffey, Photographer

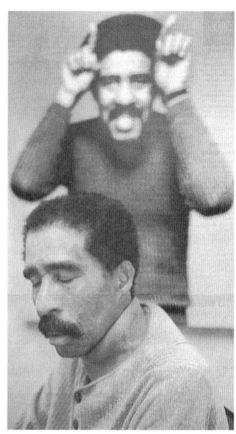

Award of Excellence
The San Diego Union-Tribune
San Diego, CA
Howard Lipin, Photographer

Award of Excellence
The San Diego Union-Tribune
San Diego, CA
John Gastaldo, Photographer

Concord Monitor
Concord, NH
Dan Habib, Photographer;
John Kaplan, Designer;
Charlotte Thibault, Artist

TEEN SEXUALITY

in a culture

of confusion

A DOCUMENTARY STUDY BY DAN HABIB

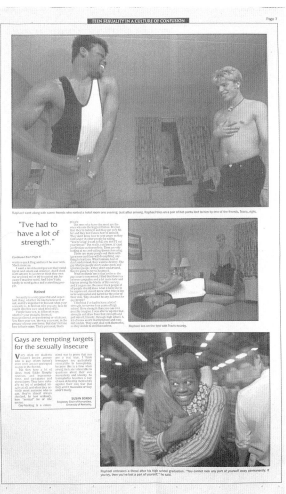

Raphael went along with some friends who rented a hotel room one evening. Just after arriving, Raphael tries on a pair of hot-pants lent to him by one of the friends, Travis, right.

"I've had to
have a lot of
strength."

Raphael lies on the bed with Travis nearby.

Gays are tempting targets for the sexually insecure

SUSAN BORDO
Singletary Chair of Humanities,
University of Kentucky.

Raphael embraces a friend after his high school graduation. "You cannot lock any part of yourself away permanently. If you try, you've lost a part of yourself," he said.

MICHAEL

"Marriage is a sacrament."

you're married, but if you are going to have sex we hope it's with someone you love, and if it is, you know, we hope you use protection.

Michael, of Manchester, and Tina, of Vermont, decided to abstain from intercourse until their wedding day.

Tina, Michael and friends let loose at their wedding reception.

As their wedding reception begins, Tina moves to embrace Michael as Tina's bridesmaids look on from the head table.

Religion can be a source of positive sexual values

RON GREEN
Professor of Religion and director
of the Ethics Institute at Dartmouth
College, author of Religion and
Moral Reason.

Michael and Tina lie on the bed at their Burlington, Vermont home on their wedding night. "When you give yourself to someone in sex, that's the ultimate act," Michael said. "If you wait until marriage, you're committing yourself to the person that you do marry on your wedding day that I've never given this part of myself to anybody before. That is the ultimate act of love."

Award of Excellence
The Philadelphia Inquirer Magazine
Philadelphia, PA
Bert Fox, Art Director/Photo Editor/Designer; Christine
Dunleavy, Design Director; April Saul, Photographer

Award of Excellence
The Philadelphia Inquirer Magazine
Philadelphia, PA
Bert Fox, Art Director/Photo Editor/Designer; Christine Dunleavy, Design Director; April Saul, Photographer

TRAINING AT TIGER CAMP

STORY AND PHOTOGRAPHS BY CHRISTOPHE LOVINY AND THIERRY FALISE

TO PROTECT HIS OPIUM FIELDS IN THE "GOLDEN TRIANGLE," THE WORLD'S MOST NOTORIOUS DRUG LORD GROWS HIS OWN ARMY.

IN THE THICK DAWN MIST, A boy coughs.

It is the only sound that disturbs the morning stillness as the flag of the self-proclaimed Shan state is raised over a cluster of shivering 10-year-olds standing at attention.

These are the Young Braves of Tiger Camp, new recruits for the army of drug warlord Khun Sa, the man responsible for more than a quarter of the heroin smuggled into the United States. Under indictment in the United States for heroin trafficking, described by former Attorney General Dick Thornburgh as the "Prince of Death," Khun Sa controls the most productive opium-growing region in the world, a fertile vastness in the heart of Southeast Asia's Golden Triangle.

He is estimated to have made $100 million last year exporting heroin, most of it destined for the United States' 600,000 addicts. The high-grade heroin, favored because it can be inhaled rather than injected, is contributing to a sharp rise in fatal overdoses in the U.S., including one last month in Wilmington, Del.

Khun Sa defends his booming cottage-state in the Himalayan foothills with sophisticated missiles, satellite technology and 20,000 soldiers. Here at his capital of Ho-Mong, he trains his newest troops. The young "cadets" by the flagpole, outfitted in new large uniforms and green Chinese sneakers, are the next generation of warriors.

Usually, at this time of the morning, thousands of adult soldiers fill the plain, marching, exercising, drilling. But many of the troops are now off battling the Burmese army, and the capital is under the guard of the Young Braves.

After the flag raising and morning inspection, the child soldiers, with their shaved heads and earnest faces, begin their training. With antique rifles and wooden guns, they mount an assault on an invisible enemy. They practice close-combat maneuvers. They stage a dramatic "victory." Then it's time for breakfast, followed by school.

Many of the boys who take up arms for Khun Sa are like 9-year-old Sai Ai, from the nearby village of Mae Ark. His parents, where only income is from growing opium, sent him to Tiger Camp six months ago because they couldn't feed all their children.

"My family is very poor. Some days we had only one bowl of rice," says Sai Ai. "So my father decided to send me here to become a soldier."

Far now at least, Sai Ai says his life is better away from home. He eats regularly, he has three blankets to call his own, and he attends daily classes taught by Khun Sa's soldier-instructors. "I have enough food, a better education and many friends," Sai Ai says. He says his parents occasionally make the day-long trek from their village to visit him, "but many of my friends come from very far away, so they never see their families."

Khun Sa's child army is filled with orphans and abandoned children who are among the chief casualties of the ongoing guerrilla war with the Burmese government. Eight-year-old Myn Aw, who, like most of his elders, wears a Burmese amulet around his neck to ward off enemy bullets, remembers that when he fled his village, "I saw people dying in front of me, I was shaking and crying. The Burmese were cruel. They killed people and animals."

Some of the children at Tiger Camp were *continued on next page*

THIERRY FALISE AND CHRISTOPHE LOVINY are photojournalists based in Paris.

A Tiger Camp drill instructor inspects his young troops, adjusting a cadet's stance (left). Drug warlord Khun Sa (top) proclaims himself a latter-day Robin Hood, protecting his people with profits from the local opium crop (inset).

INQUIRER 19

Award of Excellence
• Also Award of Excellence for Photojournalism Portfolio
The Philadelphia Inquirer Magazine
Philadelphia, PA
Bert Fox, Art Director/Photo Editor/Designer; Christine Dunleavy, Design Director; Michael S. Wirtz, Photographer; Sue Syrnick, Designer; Ron Cortes, Photographer; Michael Bryant, Photographer; Eric Mencher, Photographer; Christophe Loviny, Photographer; Thierry Falise, Photographer; Charles Fox, Photographer

The Young Braves (above) parade before the adult army, whose ranks they will join when they turn 16. Regular meals (right) are one of Tiger Camp's primary lures for the sons of impoverished Burmese peasants.

The opium poppy fields of the Golden Triangle (above) provide much of the heroin for American addicts. The boy soldiers who will protect the drug fields drop their guard (left) during a playful moment at Tiger Camp. ⬛

INSIDE: GIVING THE GIFT OF LIFE TO YOURSELF
INQUIRER
January 22, 1995
The Philadelphia Inquirer Magazine

PHOTOGRAPHY BY RON CORTES

urban voodoo

A PHILADELPHIA MAMBO INVOKES THE ANCIENT SPIRITS OF HAITI.

Award of Excellence
• Also Award of Excellence for Magazine Cover
The Philadelphia Inquirer Magazine
Philadelphia, PA
Bert Fox, Art Director/Photo Editor & Designer; Christine Dunleavy, Design Director; Ron Cortes, Photographer

Award of Excellence
Telegraph Herald
Dubuque, IA
David Guralnick,
Photographer; Mark Hirsch,
Photo Manager/Design; Mike
Day, Editorial Artist/Design;
Susan B. Gwiasda, Reporter

A Heart for
Heather

Stories by Susan B. Gwiasda • Photos by David Guralnick
of the Telegraph Herald

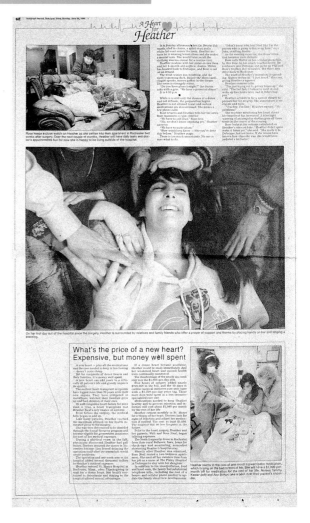

What's the price of a new heart? Expensive, but money well spent

Award of Excellence
• Also Award of Excellence for Special News Topics
The Times-Picayune
New Orleans, LA
Tyrone Turner, Photographer; Doug Parker,
Photo Editor; George Berke, Design Director

LIFE IN A TEEN GANG

DANGEROUS BONDS

They've always been with us,

groups of bored suburban teen-agers attracting mischief. But in the suburbs today, some teens are forming more dangerous bonds. In Jefferson Parish, officials who long denied the problem now estimate gang membership at perhaps 600 to 1,000. One in Metairie calls itself the Piru Bloods. At a distance, their members seem more bluster than menace. But a close look inside gang life reveals disaffected youths with an attitude — and sometimes the guns to back it up. Mix in drugs, alcohol and a long, hot summer, and gatherings become gasoline looking for a match.

A NEED FOR
ACCEPTANCE, A-17

CROSSING
THE LINE, A-19

BOREDOM AND
BRAGGADOCIO, A-18

THOUGH THEY
SAY MOST OF
THEIR FIGHTS
ARE WITH
THEIR FISTS,
Piru gang members Brian, 19,
and "Monkey,"
17, handle
loaded semiautomatics
brought to a
Metairie Carnival parade, "for
protection."
Most gang
members in this
report agreed to
talk and be photographed on
condition that
their full names
not be published.

By TYRONE
TURNER
Staff photographer
and
LYNNE JENSEN
Staff writer

STORIES BEGIN ON A-17

LIFE IN A TEEN GANG

"Something needs to be done because people are getting fed up with it. We need to do more in the home, but the police need to do more on the street, too. And that's not just pulling the kids on the side and . . . hitting them on the head with the billy club. They need to listen to them." — Kathy Pollet, mother of Piru gang leader.

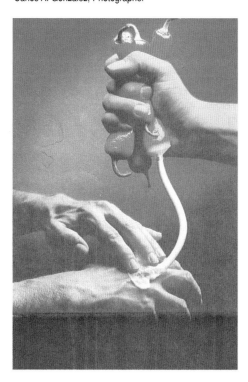

Award of Excellence
Los Angeles Times
Los Angeles, CA
Robert Gauthier, Photographer/Illustrator; Janis Sih, Art Director & Designer

Award of Excellence
The Washington Post
Washington, DC
Kelly Doe, Art Director & Designer; Polly Becker, Photo Illustrator

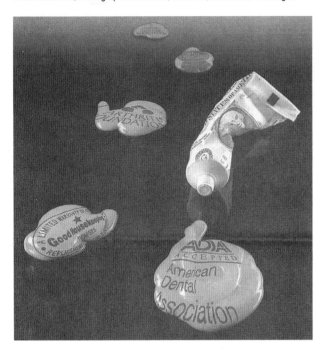

Award of Excellence
St. Louis Post-Dispatch
St Louis, MO
Tom Borgman, Graphics Editor; Jerry Naunheim Jr.,
Photographer

Award of Excellence
The Fresno Bee
Fresno, CA
John Walker, Photographer

Award of Excellence
The News Tribune
Tacoma, WA
Dean J. Koepfler, Photographer

Award of Excellence
The Palm Beach Post
West Palm Beach, FL
Allen Eyestone, Photographer; Pete Cross, Photo Director; Mark Edelson, Photo Editor; Jeff Greene, Photo Editor

Award of Excellence
The Press Democrat
Santa Rosa, CA
John Burgess, Photographer

Award of Excellence
The Palm Beach Post
West Palm Beach, FL
Allen Eyestone, Photographer; Pete Cross, Photo Editor; Mark Edelson, Photo Editor; Jeff Greene, Photo Editor; Gary Kanadjian, Photographer; E.A. Kennedy III, Photographer; John J. Lopinot, Photographer; Mark Mirko, Photographer; Lannis Waters, Photographer

9

Included in this category were charted information, graphs, diagrams and maps with or without the use of illustration or photography. Portfolios must have included six pieces of work entered in one of two divisions: Work by one artist, work by more than one artist.

Informational Graphics

- Breaking News
- Portfolio
- Black & White and/or One Color
- Two or More colors

Gold

The Dallas Morning News

Dallas, TX

Ben McConnell, Deputy Art Director; Laurie Burns, Edition Supervisor; Kathleen Vincent, Art Director; Alison Hamilton, Designer; Steve Kenny, Reporter; Don Huff, Illustrator; Chris Morris, Illustrator; Lon Tweeten, Illustrator

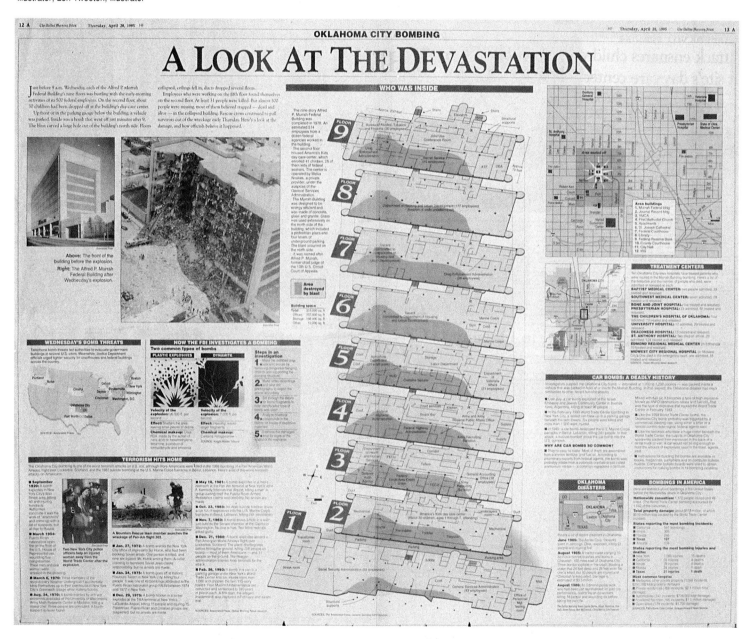

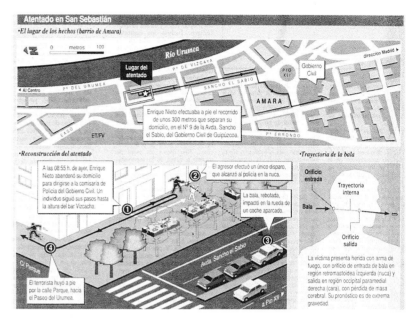

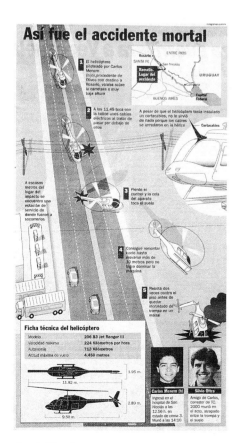

Award of Excellence
Detroit Free Press
Detroit, MI
Laura Varon Brown, Graphics Director; Marty Westman, Artist/Illustrator; Hank Szerlag, Artist/Illustrator

Award of Excellence
The New York Times
New York, NY
John Papasian, Illustrator; Ty Ahmad-Taylor, Graphics Editor

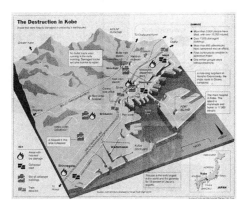

Award of Excellence
The Seattle Times
Seattle, WA
Bo Hok Cline, News Graphic Designer; David Miller, Art Director

Award of Excellence
The Marin Independent Journal
Novato, CA
Michael Jantze, Senior Graphic Artist

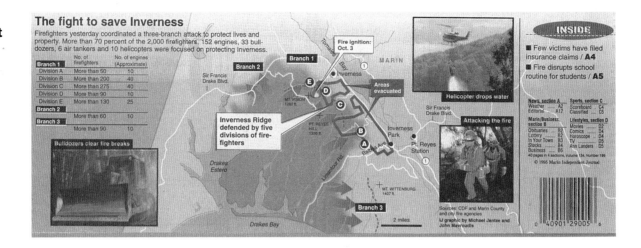

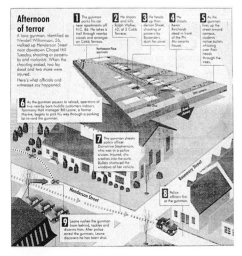

Award of Excellence
The News & Observer
Raleigh, NC
Charles Apple, Illustrator/Reporter; Nam Nguyen, Illustrator; Woody Vondracek, Illustrator; Ken Mowry, Graphics Director; David Pickel, Presentation/Design Editor

Award of Excellence
The Cincinnati Enquirer
Cincinnati, OH
John Humenik, Graphics Editor; David Aikins, Artist; News Staff

Award of Excellence
Reforma
México City, Mexico
José Luis Barros, Jorge Peñaloza, Israel Mejía, Illustrators; Daniel Esqueda, Section Designer; Agustin Marquez, Photo.; Ma. Luisa Díaz de Léon, Ed.; Arturo Jimenez, Graphics Ed.; Emilio Deheza, Art Director; Eduardo Danilo, Design Consultant

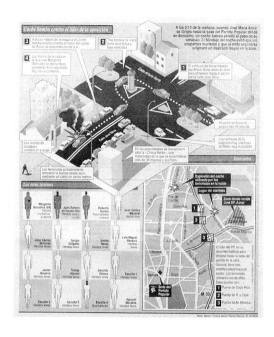

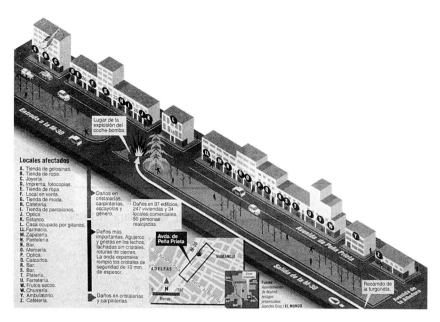

Atentado en Loyola

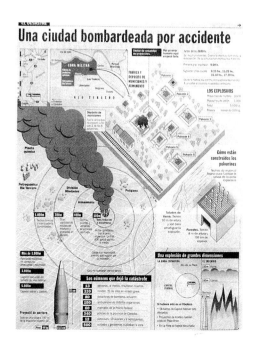

1 14:26 h.
El brigada del Ejército Mariano de Juan salió del acuartelamiento del barrio de Loyola de San Sebastián (al otro lado del puente que cruza sobre el río Urumea) vestido de paisano, con chándal y zapatillas deportivas.

2 Tras atravesar el puente, el brigada cruzó la calle y caminó hacia su domicilio, situado a unos 500 metros del cuartel.

4 Uno de los activistas se acercó por detrás a Mariano de Juan y efectuó un único disparo sobre su nuca, causándole la muerte en el acto.

3 14:27 h.
Dos individuos descendieron a cara descubierta de un Fiat Tipo blanco. Un tercer terrorista permaneció en el vehículo.

5 Los dos terroristas subieron en el coche y se dieron a la fuga en dirección a San Sebastián. El vehículo apareció minutos después en el Paseo del Urumea de la capital guipuzcoana.

Silver
El Mundo
Madrid, Spain
Mario Tascón, Infographics Editor; Modesto J. Carrasco, Artist; Juancho Cruz, Artist; Rafael Ferrer, Artist; Beatriz Eguarras, Artist; Rafael Estrada, Artist; Chema Matía, Artist; Ramón Ramos, Artist; Dina Sánchez, Artist; Juan Velasco, Artist

Una ciudad bombardeada por accidente

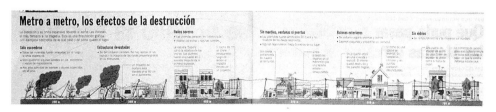

Metro a metro, los efectos de la destrucción

Award of Excellence
Clarin
Buenos Aires, Argentina
Gerardo Morel, Artist; Jaime Serra, Artist & Graphics Editor; Xavier Conesa, Art Director; Hector Ceballos, Artist; Jorge Donaiger, Artist; Andrea Tozzini, Artist

Award of Excellence
The Orange County Register
Santa Ana, CA
Paul Carbo, Artist; Monica Edwards, Artist; Robin Mills-Murphy, Artist; Craig Pursley, Artist; George Turney, Artist; James Zisk, Artist; Mary Zisk, Artist; Chris Boucly, Graphics Reporter; Bill Cunningham, Designer; Karen Kelso, Designer

Award of Excellence
The New York Times
New York, NY
Graphics Staff

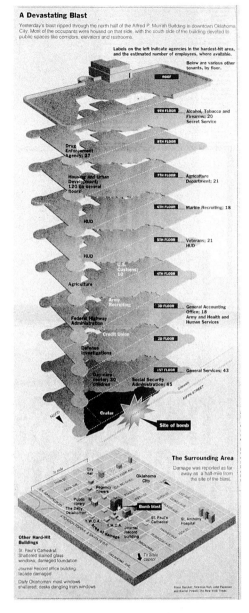

Award of Excellence
Clarin
Buenos Aires, Argentina
Jaime Serra, Artist & Graphics Editor; Xavier Conesa, Art Director; Hector Ceballos, Artist

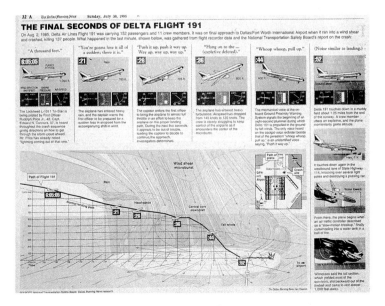

Award of Excellence
The Dallas Morning News
Dallas, TX
Lon Tweeten, Artist; Ben McConnell, Deputy Art Director; Kathleen Vincent, Art Director

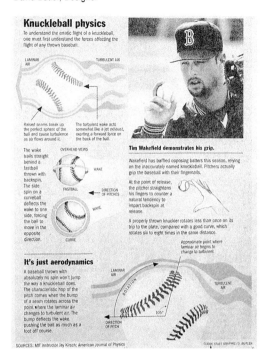

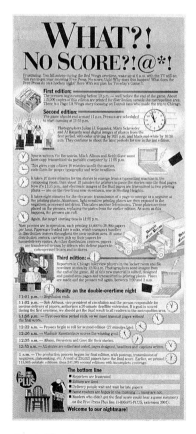

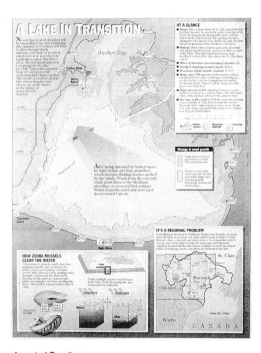

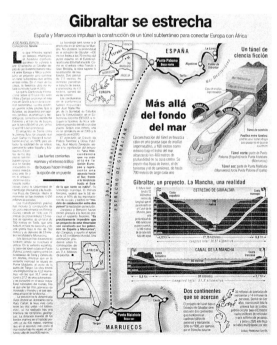

Award of Excellence
The New York Times
New York, NY
Charles M. Blow, Illustrator/Graphics Editor; Michael
Valenti, Art Director

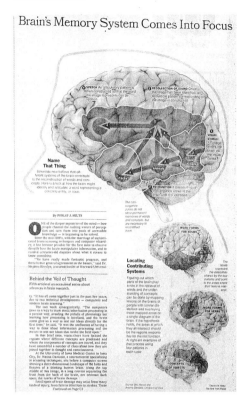

Award of Excellence
The New York Times
New York, NY
Ty Ahmad-Taylor, Graphics Editor

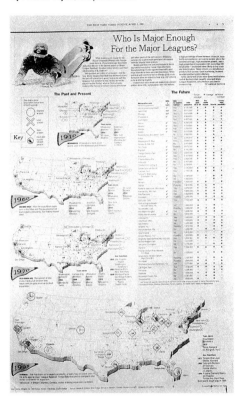

Award of Excellence
The Washington Post
Washington, DC
Laura Stanton, Graphic Artist, Designer; Jackson Dykman,
Assistant Art Director

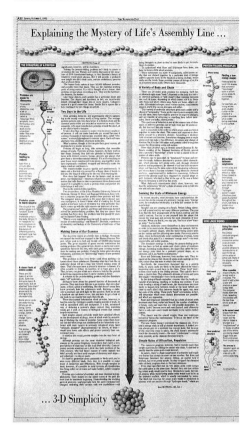

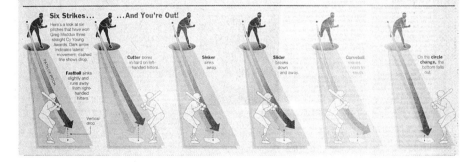

Award of Excellence
The New York Times
New York, NY
Megan Jaegerman, Illustrator; Joe Ward, Graphics Editor

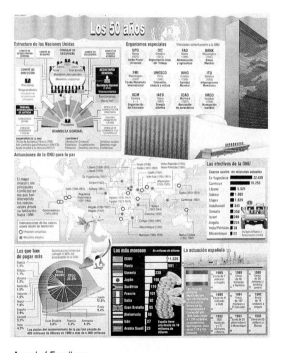

Award of Excellence
El Periódico de Catalunya
Barcelona, Spain
Jordi Català, Author/Infographic Editor

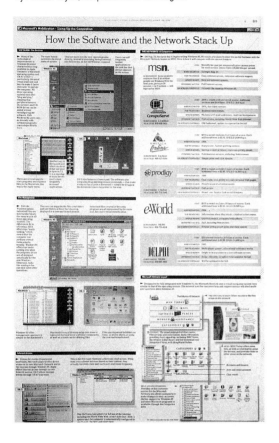

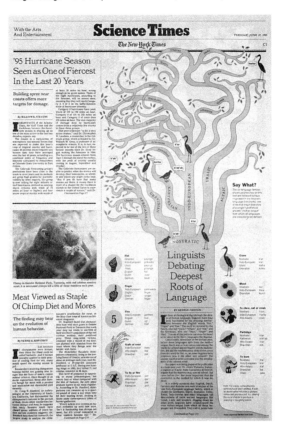

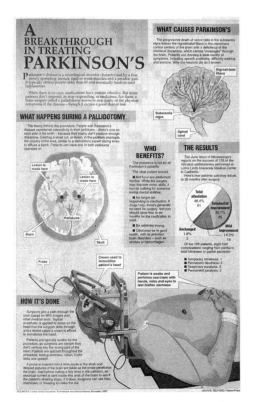

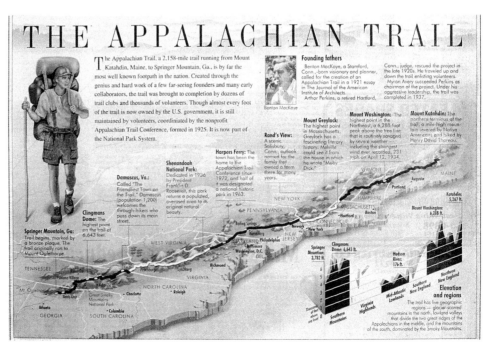

Award of Excellence
The Orange County Register
Santa Ana, CA
Paul Carbo, Artist, Designer & Reporter; Tia Lai, Visuals Editor

Award of Excellence
The San Diego Union-Tribune
San Diego, CA
Paul Horn, Graphics Journalist

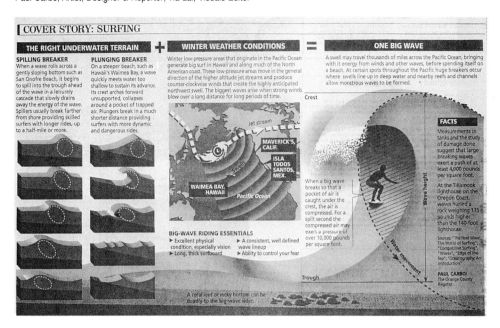

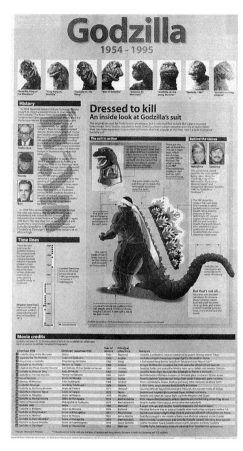

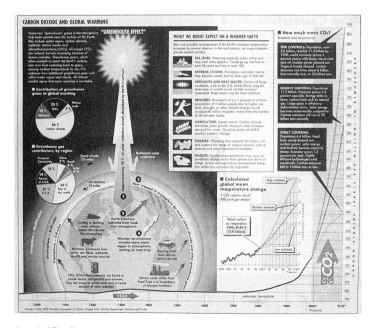

Award of Excellence
The San Francisco Chronicle
San Francisco, CA
John Blanchard, Designer/Illustrator

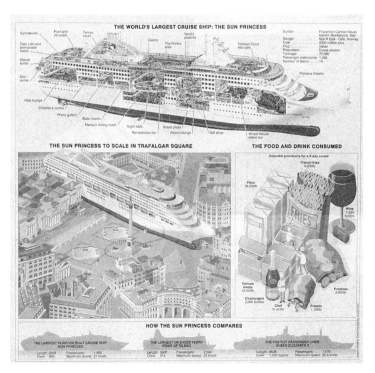

Award of Excellence
The Times
London, England
Geoffrey Sims, Artist; Tony Garrett, Artist

Silver
• Also Award of Excellence for Portfolio
Clarin
Buenos Aires, Argentina
Jaime Serra, Graphics Editor; Xavier Conesa, Art Director

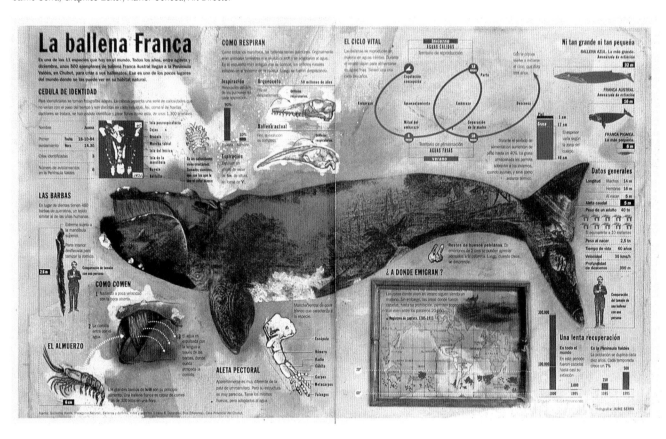

Silver
El Mundo
Madrid, Spain
Jorge Fernandez, Infographics Artist; DPI, Infographics Artist

Award of Excellence
The Boston Globe
Boston, MA
Cindy Daniels, Editorial Designer; Richard Sanchez,
Informational Graphics Designer

Award of Excellence
El Periódico de Catalunya
Barcelona, Spain
Ramon Curto, Author; Jordi Català, Infographic Editor

Award of Excellence
The News & Observer
Raleigh, NC
Nam Nguyen, Illustrator; Ken Mowry, Graphics Director;
David Pickel, Presentation/Design Editor

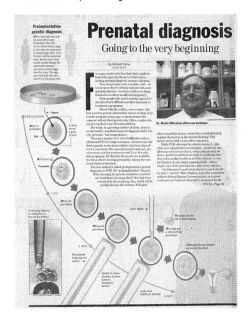

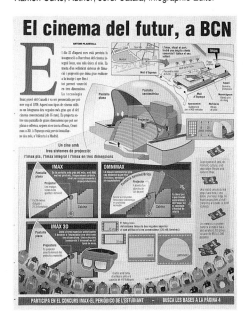

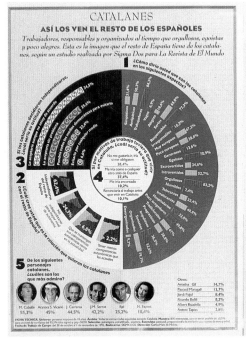

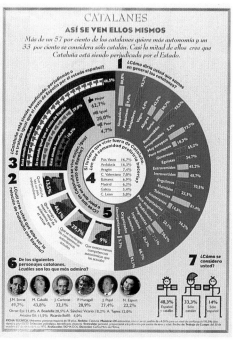

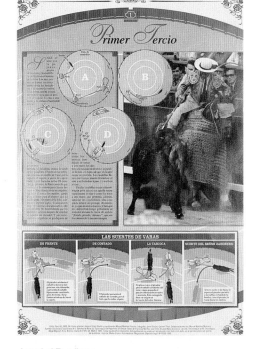

Award of Excellence
El Mundo
Madrid, Spain
Juancho Cruz, Artist

Award of Excellence
El Pais
Madrid, Spain
Javier Sicilia, Graphic Journalist; Carmen Trejo, Graphic
Journalist

Award of Excellence
Los Angeles Times/Orange County Edition
Costa Mesa, CA
Scott Brown, Artist, Writer & Researcher; Karen
Dardick, Writer & Researcher; Tom Reinken, Deputy
Graphics Editor; Kris Onuigbo, Art Director

Award of Excellence
Los Angeles Times/Orange County Edition
Costa Mesa, CA
Scott Brown, Artist, Writer & Researcher; Karen
Dardick, Writer & Researcher; Tom Reinken, Deputy
Graphics Editor; Kris Onuigbo, Art Director

Award of Excellence
The News-Sentinel
Fort Wayne, IN
Rich Griffis, PrepSports Editor; Kevin Harreld, Copy Editor; Ezra Wolfe, Designer; Cindy Jones-
Hulfachor, Graphic Reporter; Brian Tombaugh, Photographer

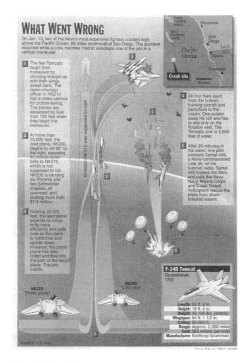

Award of Excellence
The San Diego Union-Tribune
San Diego, CA
Paul Horn, Graphics Journalist

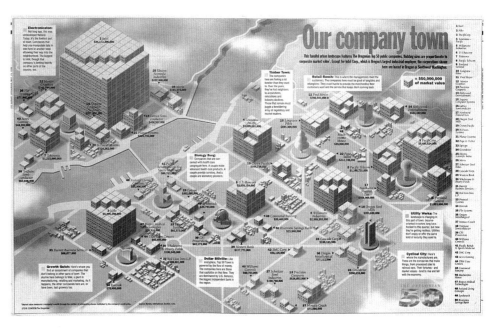

Award of Excellence
The Oregonian
Portland, OR
Steve Cowden, Artist; Michelle Wise, Graphics Director

Award of Excellence
The Philadelphia Inquirer
Philadelphia, PA
Cristina Rivero, Artist

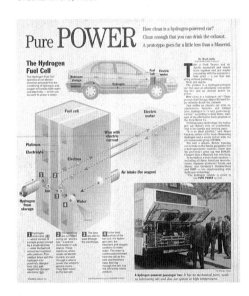

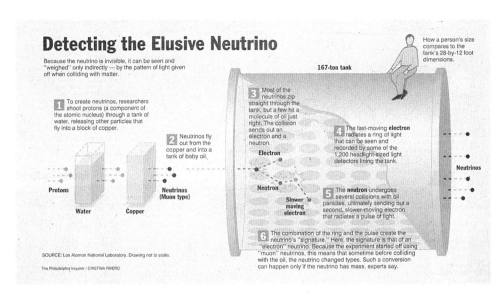

Award of Excellence
Star Tribune
Minneapolis, MN
Sidney Jablonski, Artist/Designer/Researcher; David Silk, Artist; Greg Branson, Researcher;
Tim Campbell, Graphics Editor; Anders Ramberg, Art Director

Award of Excellence
The Washington Post
Washington, DC
Laura Stanton, Graphic Artist, Designer; Jackson Dykman, Researcher, Writer & Designer;
Richard Furno, Cartographer

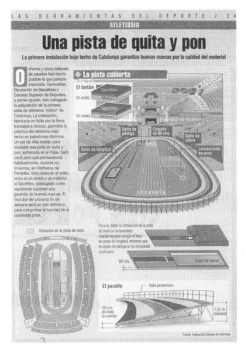

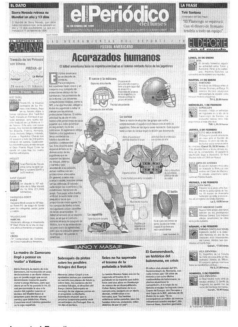

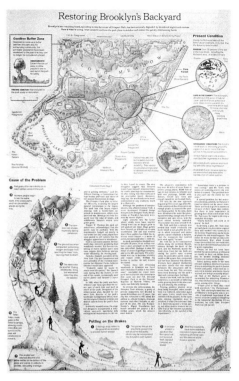

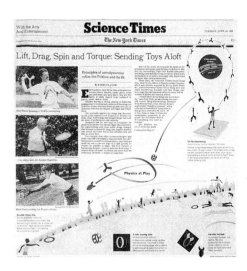

Award of Excellence
Expansion
Madrid, Spain
Jose Juan Gamez, Design Director; Pablo Ma Ramirez, Graphic Artist; Antonio Martin Hervas, Graphic Artist; Juan de Dios Ferreira, Graphic Artist

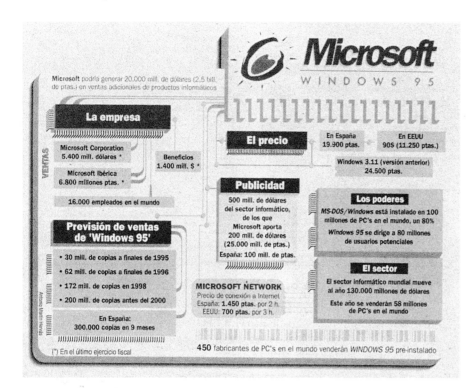

Award of Excellence
The New York Times
New York, NY
Ty Ahmad-Taylor, Graphics Editor

Silver

El Mundo

Madrid, Spain

Mario Tascón, Infographics Editor; Modesto J. Carrasco, Artist; Juancho Cruz, Artist; Chema Matía, Artist; Ramón Ramos, Artist; Gorka Sampedro, Artist; Dina Sánchez, Artist; Juan Velasco, Artist; Pedro Velasco, Artist; Juan Santiuste, Artist

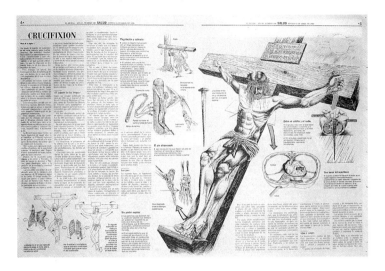

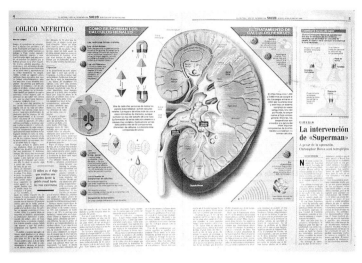

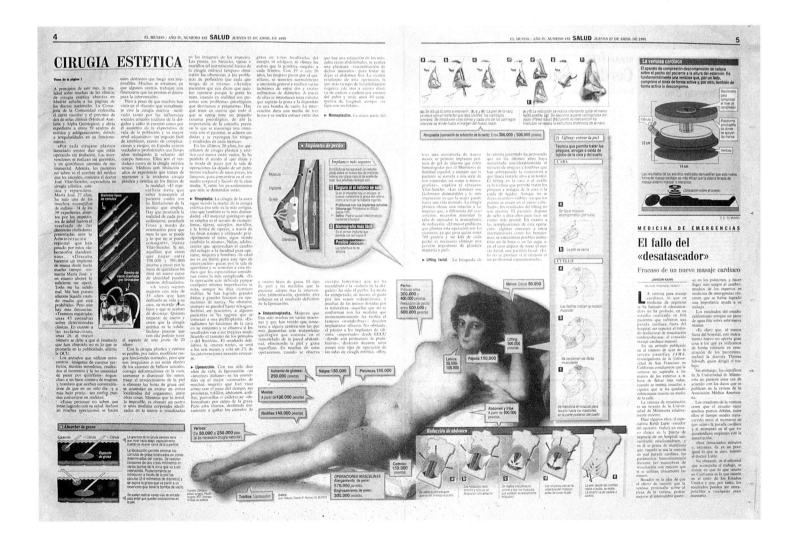

Award of Excellence
• Also Award of Excellence for Business Page

Expansion
Madrid, Spain

Jose Juan Gamez, Design Director; Pablo Ma Ramirez, Graphic Artist; Antonio Martin Hervas, Graphic Artist; Mar Domingo, Graphic Artist; Bianca Serrano, Graphic Artist

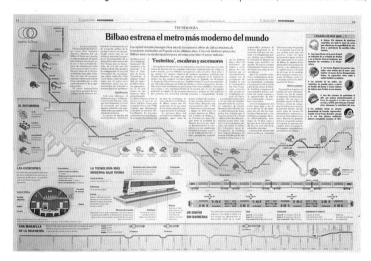

Award of Excellence

Marca
Madrid, Spain

José Juan Gámez, Design Director; Pablo Ma Ramírez, Graphic Artist; Mar Domingo, Graphic Artist; Cesar Galera, Graphic Artist; Martina Gil, Graphic Artist; Sofia Valganon, Graphic Artist; Bianca Serrano, Graphic Artist; Miguel A. Fernandez, Graphic Artist

10

Entries that did not fit in one of the 21 categories in this competition could be included in miscellaneous. Also, included in this chapter are redesigns and reprints as well as brief biographies of the 21 judges who had to make the tough decisions as to the 17th Edition winners. Finally, every possible effort was made to provide a complete, correct index of winning publications and the names of the individuals responsible as listed on the entry forms.

Miscellaneous

- Redesign
- Reprints
- Judges
- Index

Before

Silver

Centre Daily Times

State College, PA
Cecil Bentley, Executive
Editor; Deborah Withey, Art
Director & Designer; Design
Staff

After

Award of Excellence

The Atlanta Journal and Constitution

Atlanta, GA
Tony DeFeria, Design Director; Sheri Taylor, Art Director;
Ellen Voss, News Desk Design Manager; D.W. Pine,
Design Coordinator; Layout Staff Photo Staff Ron Martin,
Editor; John Walter, ME

Before

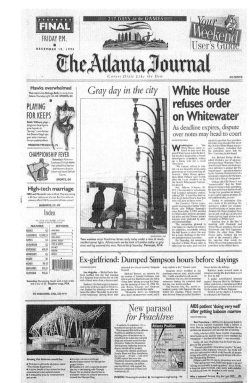

After

Before

After

Before

After

Before

After

Award of Excellence
Ocala Star-Banner
Ocala, Fl
Steve Antley, Graphics Editor; John MacLeod, Design Consultant

Before

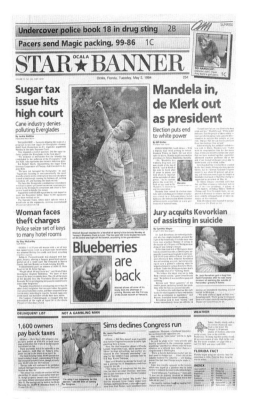

Before

After

Before

After

Award of Excellence
The Spokesman-Review
Spokane, WA
John K. Nelson, Design Editor; Scott Sines, Managing Editor, visuals

Award of Excellence
Anchorage Daily News
Anchorage, AK
Galie Jean-Louis, Features Design Director; Kevin Ellis, Designer; Lance Lekander, Designer; Pamela Dunlap-Shohl, Designer

Before

After

Before

Before

After

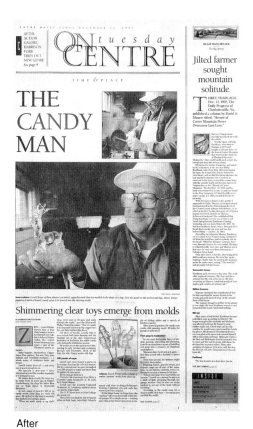

After

Award of Excellence
The Charlotte Observer
Charlotte, NC
Rob Covey, Redesign Consultant; Scott Goldman, Sports Design Editor; Monica Moses, Design Director; Brenda Pinnell, Redesign Coordinator; Sports Staff

Before

After

Before

After

Award of Excellence
Detroit Free Press Magazine
Chicago, IL
Claire Innes, Art Director; J. Kyle Keener, Photographer; Peggy Castine, Deputy Editor; Wendy W. Keebler, Deputy Editor; Brian Dickerson, Editor

Award of Excellence
The Home News & Tribune
East Brunswick, NJ
Mary Clark Ladd, Designer; Harris Siegel, ME/Design & Photography; Teresa Klink, ME/News; Dick Hughes, Editor; Tom Kerr, Art Director; Mary Price, Design Section Editor

Before

After

The Home News & Tribune
East Brunswick, NJ
Mary Clark Ladd, Designer; Harris Siegel, ME/Design &
Photography; Teresa Klink, ME/News; Dick Hughes,
Editor; Tom Kerr, Art Director; Steve Muoio, Designer; Amy
Catalano, Designer; Christine Birch, Designer; Joe Lee,
Designer; Linda Heyniger, Designer

Before

After

La Voz del Interior
Córdoba, Argentina
Miguel De Lorenzi, Art Director & Designer; Javier
Candellero, Designer; Oscar Beguán, Photo Editor; Staff,
Photographer; Juan Carlos Genzález, Editor; Luis León
Yong, Infographics Editor; Javier Candellero, Illustrator;
Mario García, Design Consultant; Jeff Goertzen, Graphics
Consultant

Le Soleil
Québec, Canada
Lucie Lacava, Designer; Desk Staff Gilbert Lacasse,
Editor; Majella Soucy, AME; Michel Samson, AME; Jean-
Pascal Beaupre, Front Page Designer

Before

Before

After

Before

After

Award of Excellence
Nashville Banner
Nashville, TN
Leigh Melton Singleton, Graphic Artist; Charles Arms, Designer; Mike McGehee, Design Editor; Kenny Monteith, Redesign Coordinator; Steve Caverdish, Redesign Coordinator; Pat Embry, ME

Before

After

Before

After

Award of Excellence
The Albuquerque Journal
Albuquerque, NM
Annemarie Neff, Assistant Design Director; Carolyn Flynn, AME Photo/Design; Joe Kirby, Design Director; Nancy Tripton, Access Editor; Russ Ball, Illustrator; Carol Cooperrider, Illustrator; Karen Moses, AME Features

Award of Excellence
The Charlotte Observer
Charlotte, NC
Rob Covey, Redesign Consultant; Scott Goldman, Sports Design Editor; Monica Moses, Design Director; Brenda Pinnell, Redesign Coordinator; Sports Staff

Before

After

Chicago Tribune

Chicago, IL
Staff, Rick Tuma, Artist; Steve Duenes, Artist; Sid Smith,
Writer; Nancy Watkins Wood, Editor; Bob Fila,
Photographer

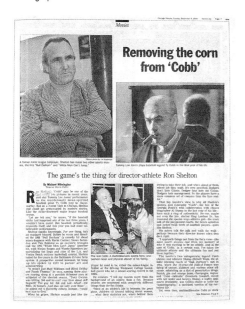

Before

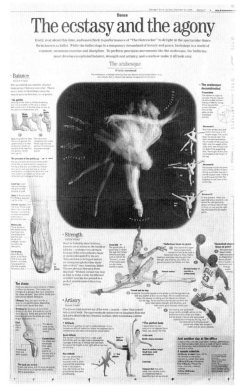

After

Before

After

The New York Times

New York, NY
Tom Bodkin, Associate ME & Design Director; John
MacLeod, Art Director; Corinne Myller, Designer

Award of Excellence

The News & Observer

Raleigh, NC
David Pickel, Presentation/Design Editor; Ken Mowry,
Graphics Director

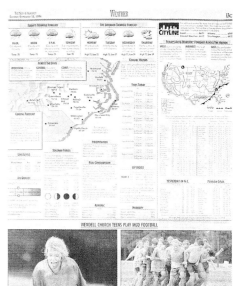

Before

After

Award of Excellence
The San Diego Union-Tribune
San Diego, CA
Bill Dawson, Designer; Stan McNeal, Sports Editor; Jess Kearney, Sports Editor; Doug Williams, Sports Editor

Award of Excellence
• Also Award of Excellence for Informational Graphics
Chicago Tribune
Chicago, IL
Stacy Sweat, Graphics Editor; Kris Goodfellow, Assistant Subject Editor; Andrew DeVigal, Graphic Artist; Steve Duenes, Graphic Artist

Before

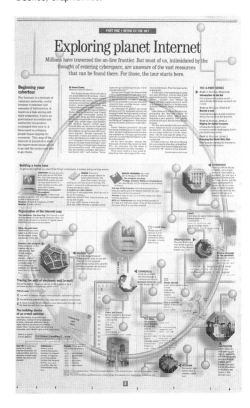

After

Before

After

Award of Excellence
Star Tribune
Minneapolis, MN
Pam Fine, News Leader; Bill Dunn, Visual Content Editor; Greg Branson, Researcher; Tim J. McGuire, Editor/General Manager RCU; Anders Ramberg, Design Director; Tim Bitney, Redesign Team Editor

Award of Excellence
Chicago Tribune
Chicago, IL
Steve Layton, Graphic Artist; Bill Hogan, Photographer; Blair Kamin, Writer

The Kansas City Star

Kansas City, KS

Jean Moxam, AME Graphics/Design

The Hartford Courant

Hartford, CT

Christian Potter Drury, Art Director & Designer; Thom McGuire, Photo Director; John Scanlan, Photo Editor; Staff

Chicago Tribune

Chicago, IL

Therese Shechter, Art Director; Theresa Badovich, Designer; Celeste Bernard, Assistant Subject Editor; Ken Marshall, Assistant Subject Editor; Stephen Ravenscraft, Graphic Artist; Steve Duenes, Graphic Artist; Dave Jahntz, Graphic Artist; Chris Walker, Photographer

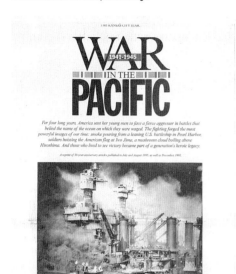

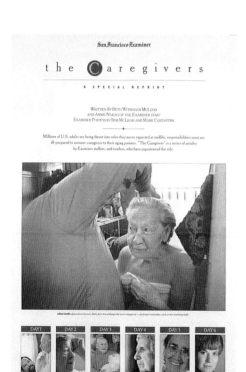

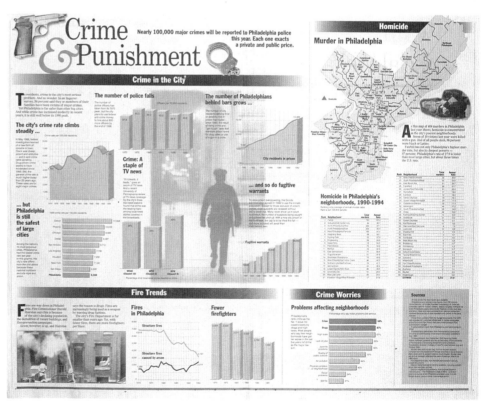

San Francisco Examiner

San Francisco, CA

Kelly Frankeny, AME Design; Bob McLeod, Photographer; Mignon Khargie, Designer; Beth Witrogen, Reporter; Mark Costantini, Photographer

The Philadelphia Inquirer

Philadelphia, PA

Cristina Rivero, Graphic Artist; Anne Bigler, Page Designer; Eric Mencher, Photographer; Bill Marsh, Design Director; Dave Milne, AME Graphics

Award of Excellence
The Philadelphia Daily News
Philadelphia, PA
John Sherlock, Graphics Editor; Peter Kohama, Illustrator; Becky Batcha, Researcher

Award of Excellence
Democrat and Chronicle
Rochester, NY
Dennis R. Floss, Section Editor & Designer; Joanne Andrews, Artist

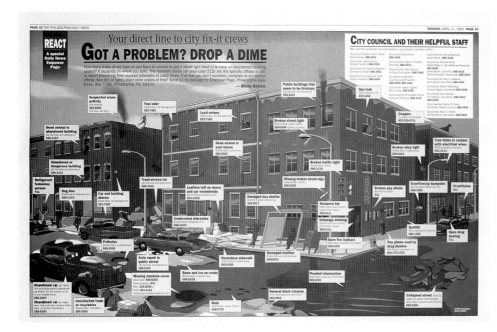

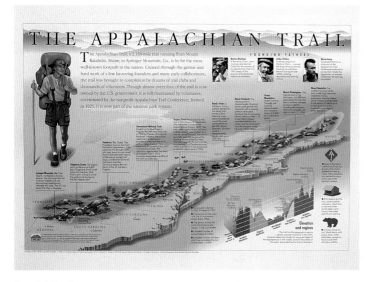

Award of Excellence
The News & Observer
Raleigh, NC
Nam Nguyen, Illustrator; Scott Huler, Researcher; David Pickel, Presentation/Design Editor; Ken Mowry, Graphics Director; Ben Estes, Editor

Award of Excellence
The News & Observer
Raleigh, NC
Charles Apple, Illustration, Design & Research; Ken Mowry, Graphics Director; David Pickel, Presentation/Design Editor

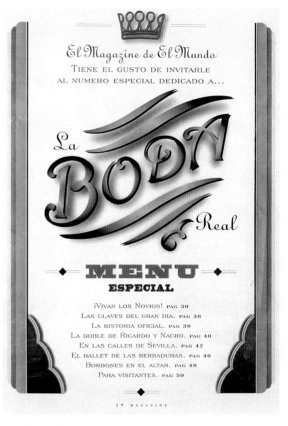

Award of Excellence
Le Soleil
Québec, Canada
Lucie Lacava, Designer; Ricardo Martinez, Illustrator; Gilbert Lacasse, Editor; Majella Soucy, AME; Michel Samson, AME

Award of Excellence
The Orange County Register
Santa Ana, CA
Bill Cunningham, Wire Editor; Nanette Bisher, AME/Art Director; Paul Carbo, Artist; Lisa Mertins, Artist; George Turney, Artist

Old

New

Award of Excellence
Tages-Anzeiger
Zürich, Switzerland
Andreas Bucher, Editor; Helmut Germer, Illustrator/Graphic Artist; Paul Kälin, Graphic Designer; Werner Keller, DME

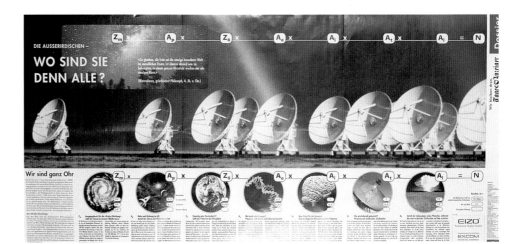

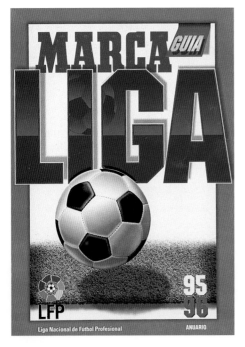

Award of Excellence
Marca
Madrid, Spain
Staff

Award of Excellence
Marca
Madrid, Spain
Staff

Two groups of judges

The first group of five judges was looking only at the competition's overall design category, studying newspapers as a whole. They determined the top overall newspapers for information and design presentation in all 20 categories of the competition in three circulation sizes. These newspapers have the distinction of being the World's Best-Designed Newspapers.

The second group of 16 judges was organized much as in past competitions: three groups of five judges with a "floater judge" to solve conflicts and act as a backup to the three groups.

Dos grupos de jueces

El primer grupo de cinco jueces sólo se ocupó de las categorías generales de diseño, estudiando los periódicos en conjunto. Escogió los periódicos cuya información y diseño eran los mejores, en las 20 categorías del concurso, en tres niveles de circulación. Estos periódicos obtuvieron la distinción de ser los periódicos mejor diseñados del mundo.

El segundo grupo de 16 jueces se organizó en una forma muy similar a la de los concursos anteriores: tres grupos de cinco jueces y un juez ad hoc, para resolver los conflictos y servir de refuerzo a los tres grupos.

Word's Best-Designed Newspapers Judges

Jueces de los periódicos mejor diseñados del mundo

Peter Bhatia, managing editor of The Oregonian, joined the Oregon newspaper in November 1993 and has since helped lead its conversion to a team-based newsroom. Before joining the newspaper, he was executive editor of The Fresno Bee. He has worked at six other newspapers during his 20 years in the newspaper business.

Peter Bhatia, editor gerente de The Oregonian, ingresó al periódico de Oregon en noviembre de 1993, y desde entonces ha contribuido a dirigir su conversión en una sala de redacción de equipo. Antes de ingresar al periódico, fue director ejecutivo de The Fresno Bee. Ha trabajado en otros seis periódicos, durante sus 20 años en la industria periodística.

Sue Dean, editor and vice president of The Sun News, joined that newspaper as managing editor in 1987 before she was promoted to her current job in 1990. Before joining the Myrtle Beach, S.C. newspaper, she spent 10 years at the Daily Camera in Boulder, Colo., working her way up from reporter to assistant managing editor.

Sue Dean, editora y vicepresidenta de The Sun News, ingresó a ese periódico como editora gerente, en 1987, antes de que se la ascendiera a su cargo actual, en 1990. Antes de ingresar al periódico de Myrtle Beach, Carolina del Sur, trabajó 10 años en el Daily Camera, en Boulder, Colorado, en donde ascendió de reportera a editora gerente auxiliar.

Bob Giles, editor and publisher of The Detroit News, joined that newspaper as executive editor in 1986. His newspaper career began in 1958 at the Akron (Ohio) Beacon Journal where he served as managing editor, then executive editor. He has served as a Pulitzer Prize juror six times since 1970.

Bob Giles, editor y de The Detroit News, ingresó a ese periódico como editor ejecutivo, en 1986. Su carrera periodística se inició en 1958, en el Beacon Journal de Akron, Ohio, en donde desempeñó el cargo de editor gerente y luego el de director ejecutivo. Ha sido jurado del premio Pulitzer seis veces, desde 1970.

Marty Petty, senior vice president and general manager of The Hartford (Conn.) Courant, was appointed to her current position in November 1994. Her responsibilities include advertising, circulation, marketing, electronic marketing, commercial sales, production, information technology, facilities management and management services. She has been at the newspaper since 1983.

Marty Petty, vice presidenta principal y gerente general de The Hartford (Conn.) Courant, fue nombrada para su cargo actual en noviembre de 1994. Sus funciones comprenden la publicidad, la circulación, el mercadeo, el mercadeo electrónico, las ventas comerciales, la producción, la tecnología de la información, la administración de instalaciones y los servicios administrativos. Ha trabajado en el periódico desde 1983.

Toni Piqué, consultant for Innovación Periodística, is the former section editor at La Vanguardia in Barcelona, Spain. He was involved in developing some new sections during a redesign in 1989. Now on leave to develop a study on newsroom organization and management, he is a consultant for 12 Latin American newspapers.

Toni Piqué, asesor de innovación periodística, es un antiguo editor de sección de La Vanguardia, de Barcelona, España. Contribuyó a diseñar nuevamente ese periódico, que comprendió secciones nuevas, en 1989. Actualmente se encuentra en licencia, para llevar a cabo un estudio de organización y administración de salas de redacción. Es asesor de 12 periódicos latinoamericanos.

Judges' Bios

Biografías de los jueces

Jay Anthony, an associate professor in the School of Journalism & Mass Communication at the University of North Carolina at Chapel Hill, teaches beginning graphic design, promotional design and information graphics. He worked in newspapers for 11 years and is currently writing a basic graphic design book.

Jay Anthony, catedrático auxiliar de la Escuela de Periodismo y Comunicación de Masas de la Universidad de Carolina del Norte en Chapel Hill, enseña nociones básicas de diseño gráfico, diseño publicitario y gráficas informativas. Ha trabajado en los periódicos durante 11 años, y actualmente está escribiendo un libro sobre las nociones básicas del diseño gráfico.

Emilio Deheza has been art director since July 1993 at Reforma, a newspaper he helped to design. He was responsible for the graphic system implementation and for the recruiting and organization of the graphic teams at this Mexico City newspaper. He opened his own graphic arts studio in 1989 after working as an editorial designer for El Norte for two years.

Emilio Deheza ha sido desde julio de 1993 director artístico de Reforma, un periódico que contribuyó a diseñar. Tuvo a su cargo la puesta en práctica del sistema gráfico y la contratación y organización de los equipos gráficos de este periódico de Ciudad de México. Abrió su propio estudio de artes gráficas en 1989, tras haber trabajado durante dos años como diseñador editorial de El Norte.

Nuri Ducassi, features design director at the San Jose Mercury News, is responsible for the design of all special sections. Before joining the California newspaper in September 1994, she spent a short time at The Hartford Courant (Conn.) and five years at the El Nuevo Herald where she redesigned its Galeria section.

Nuri Ducassi, directora de diseño de artículos de actualidad del San Jose Mercury News, tiene a su cargo el diseño de todas las secciones especiales. Antes de ingresar al periódico de California, en septiembre de 1994, trabajó durante corto tiempo en The Hartford Courant, de Connecticut, y cinco años en El Nuevo Herald, donde diseñó de nuevo la sección Galería.

Bill Dunn, visual content editor of the Star Tribune in Minneapolis, is responsible for the visual presentation of the news including the photographic, design and graphic operations. He has worked in the newspaper business for 23 years at six newspapers.

Bill Dunn, editor de contenido visual del Star Tribune de Minneápolis, tiene a su cargo la presentación visual de las noticias, incluyendo la fotografía, el diseño y las operaciones gráficas. Ha trabajado en la industria periodística durante 23 años, en seis periódicos.

Carsten Gregersen, design editor for Berlingske Tidende in Copenhagen, Denmark, has worked as a reporter, systems editor and news editor at that newspaper before his present position. Gregerson, who recently redesigned his own newspaper, has been a lecturer at IFRA and at the Graphic Arts Institute of Denmark.

Carsten Gregersen, editor de diseño del Berlingske Tidende de Copenague, Dinamarca, trabajó como reportero y editor de sistemas y noticias en ese periódico, antes de desempeñar su cargo actual. Gregerson, quien recientemente diseñó de nuevo su propio periódico, ha dictado conferencias en IFRA y en el Instituto de Artes Gráficas de Dinamarca.

Jim Jennings, SND president, is a Lexington (Ky.)-based consultant who has worked for clients in Germany, Malaysia, Thailand, South Africa and the United Kingdom. Prior to becoming a consultant, he worked as group managing editor of Thomson Regional Newspapers in London. Before that he was AME/graphics at the Herald-Leader in Lexington.

Jim Jennings, presidente de la SND, es un asesor ubicado en Lexington, Kentucky, que tiene clientes en Alemania, Malasia, Tailandia, Africa del Sur y el Reino Unido. Antes de convertirse en asesor, trabajó como editor jefe de Grupo de Thompson Regional Newspapers, en Londres. Anteriormente fue AME (editor gerente) de gráficas del Herald-Leader, en Lexington.

Wayne Kamidoi, presentation editor at The New York Times, art directs the Sunday and Monday sections, special projects and coverage. He joined The Times in November 1995. Before that he worked at the Detroit Free Press since 1988, becoming design director in October 1994.

Wayne Kamidoi, editor de presentación de The New York Times, es director artístico de las secciones del domingo y el lunes y los proyectos y coberturas especiales, Ingresó en The Times en noviembre de 1995. Anteriormente había trabajado en el Detroit Free Press desde 1988, donde se convirtió en el director de diseño, en octubre de 1994.

Mignon Khargie is art director of SALON, an internet magazine of books, arts and ideas, which was first published on line in November 1995. She came to the magazine from the San Francisco Examiner where she worked as a designer/illustrator.

Mignon Khargie es directora artística de SALON, una revista de libros, artes e ideas sobre la autopista de la información, que se publicó inicialmente por computadora en noviembre de 1995. Llegó a la revista, procedente del San Francisco Examiner, donde trabajó como diseñadora e ilustradora.

Debra Page-Trim is a designer at The Providence Journal-Bulletin where she does the design and illustration for HER's, a women's section. Before joining the Rhode Island newspaper in September 1994, she was an artist at The Hartford Courant in Connecticut for five years.

Debra Page-Trim es una diseñadora de The Providence Journal-Bulletin, donde realiza el diseño y la ilustración de HER, una sección femenina. Antes de ingresar al periódico de Rhode Island, en septiembre de 1994, fue artista de The Hartford Courant, en Connecticut, durante cinco años.

Ally Palmer, art director of The Scotsman in Edinburgh, Scotland, joined Scotsman Publications in 1989 as assistant art director of Scotland on Sunday's magazine. He became design editor of Scotland on Sunday in 1991. In 1994 he joined The Scotsman as art director.

Ally Palmer, director artístico de The Scotsman, en Edimburgo, Escocia, ingresó a Scotsman Publications en 1989, como director artístico auxiliar de la revista Scotland on Sunday. Se convirtió en editor de diseño de Scotland on Sunday en 1991. En 1994 ingresó a The Scotsman, como director artístico.

Gary Piccirillo, assistant graphics editor at the Democrat and Chronicle, is primarily responsible for the design of Page 1A as well as special projects. Before joining the Rochester, N.Y. newspaper in June 1995, he spent 15 years at the Auburn (N.Y.) Citizen serving as a sports writer, sports editor and, during the last three years, AME for design.

Gary Piccirillo, editor gráfico auxiliar del Democrat y el Chronicle, está encargado principalmente del diseño de la página 1A y de los proyectos especiales. Antes de ingresar al periódico de Rochester, N.Y., en Junio de 1955, trabajó 15 años en el Auburn Citizen, Nueva York, como escritor deportivo, editor deportivo y durante los últimos tres años AME de diseño.

Tracy Porter, projects designer at The Virginian-Pilot since May 1995, is responsible for designing advance projects and Sunday's Page 1A. Before joining the Norfolk newspaper, she worked on six newspapers in the areas of copy editing and presentation design.

Tracy Porter, diseñadora de proyectos de The Virginian-Pilot desde mayo de 1995, tiene a su cargo el diseño de proyectos de vanguardia en la página 1A de la edición dominical. Antes de ingresar al periódico de Norfolk, trabajó en seis periódicos, en las áreas de corrección de manuscritos y diseño de la presentación.

Kathy Silverberg is executive editor of the TimesDaily where she has been since August 1994. Before joining the Florence, Ala. newspaper, she was editor at The Courier (Houma, La.) and the Daily Comet (Thibodaux, La.), all New York Times newspapers.

Kathy Silverberg es directora ejecutiva de The TimesDaily, en donde ha trabajado desde agosto de 1994. Antes de ingresar al periódico de Florence, Alabama, fue editora de The Courier, en Houma, Luisiana, y del Daily Comet, en Thibodaux, Luisiana, todos ellos del New York Times.

Dan Suwyn, managing editor of the Savannah (La.) News-Press, has been a reporter, projects editor, copy desk chief and presentation editor for newspapers in Delaware, Wisconsin, Maryland and Indiana. He helped launch two Sunday newspapers and redesigned The News-Sentinel in Fort Wayne, Ind.

Dan Suwyn, editor gerente del Savannah News-Press de Luisiana, ha sido reportero, editor de proyectos, jefe de redacción y editor de presentación de periódicos de Delaware, Winsconsin, Maryland e Indiana. Contribuyó al lanzamiento de dos periódicos dominicales y diseñó de nuevo el The News-Sentinel de Fort Wayne, Indiana.

Stacy Sweat, graphics editor of the Chicago Tribune, oversees the design direction and news graphics for the newspaper. As art director she supervised the redesigned the St. Paul (Minn.) Pioneer Press in 1990 and has worked on two other newspapers in many roles including staff artist, assistant systems editor and art director.

Stacy Sweat, editora gráfica del Chicago Tribune, supervisa la dirección de diseño y gráficas informativas del periódico. Como Directora Artística supervisó el nuevo St. Paul Pioneer Press de Minnesota, en 1990, y ha trabajado en otros dos periódicos, en diversos cargos, incluyendo el de artista interna, editora auxiliar de sistemas y directora artística.

Kathleen Vincent, art director at The Dallas Morning News, is responsible for feature pages design, special news design, graphics reporting, information graphics, illustration and photo styling. She received a 1994 Pulitzer Prize for her design work and graphics direction on a 14-part series titled "Violence Against Women: A Question of Human Rights."

Kathleen Vincent, directora artística de The Dallas Morning News, tiene a su cargo el diseño de las páginas de actualidad, las noticias especiales, los reportes gráficos, las gráficas informativas, la ilustración y el estilo del diseño fotográfico. En 1994 recibió un premio Pulitzer, por su trabajo de diseño y dirección gráfica en una serie de 14 partes, titulada "La violencia contra la mujer: una cuestión de derechos humanos."